THE CONGRESS

American Government

The Congress

**Carl R. Green, Ph.D.,
and William R. Sanford, Ph.D.**

SANDUSKY LIBRARY

The Rourke Corporation, Inc.

Copyright 1990 by The Rourke Corporation, Inc.

All rights reserved. No part of this book may be reproduced or utilized in any form or by any means, electronic or mechanical, including photocopying, recording or by any information storage and retrieval system without permission from the publisher.

The Rourke Corporation, Inc.
P.O. Box 3328, Vero Beach, FL 32964

Green, Carl R.
  The Congress / by Carl R. Green and William R. Sanford.
    p.   cm. — (American government)
    Summary: Describes the work of a congressman from getting elected to his duties as a member of the House of Representatives.
    ISBN 0-86593-083-X
    1. United States. Congress—Juvenile literature. [1. United States. Congress.]
I. Sanford, William R. (William Reynolds), 1927- . II. Title. III. Series.
JK1061.G67   1990
328.73—dc20   90-8638
                                                                                                                                CIP
                                                                                                                                 AC

Series Editor: Gregory Lee
Editors: Elizabeth Sirimarco, Marguerite Aronowitz
Book design and production: The Creative Spark,
  Capistrano Beach, CA
Cover photograph: Art Stein/Photo Researchers, Inc.

Authors' Note

All descriptions of the workings of the American Government that appear in this book are authentic, as are the citations of historical figures and events. Only the characters who carry the story line are fictional—and we have modeled them as closely as possible upon their real-life counterparts.

Table of Contents

1. Getting Elected Comes First — 8
2. A Lawmaker Needs Plenty Of Help — 18
3. You Can't Ignore Your Constituents — 30
4. Learning The Dimensions Of A New Job — 40
5. A Congressman's Work Is Never Done — 52
6. Only A Few Bills Survive To Become Laws — 62
7. The Struggle To Be An Honest Politician — 72
8. The Race For Reelection — 82

Glossary — 90

Bibliography — 93

Index — 94

1

Getting Elected Comes First

Phones were ringing in the busy Hillsboro real estate office, but Dick Stockton didn't seem to notice. He was tilted back in his chair, staring at the ceiling. Other realtors tiptoed past the sales manager and wondered what he had on his mind.

Dick's mind was whirling with plans, but they didn't involve real estate deals. After a late-night talk with his wife Judith, Dick had decided to go for the biggest sales project of his life. He was going to run for Congress!

As a high school senior, Dick had run for student body president. To his surprise, he'd beaten the football captain in a close election. Holding an office had taught him to respect the strengths and weaknesses of the democratic political system. In college, he'd served on the student council. And he'd been doing "get-out-the-vote" work for his party ever since moving to Hillsboro.

The idea of running for public office had first occurred to Dick a year ago. His party's county committee had asked him to run for a seat on the Hillsboro city council. Dick had turned down the offer, but the idea didn't go away. Now, to everyone's surprise, Congressman Bannister had announced he was retiring at the end of his term. With

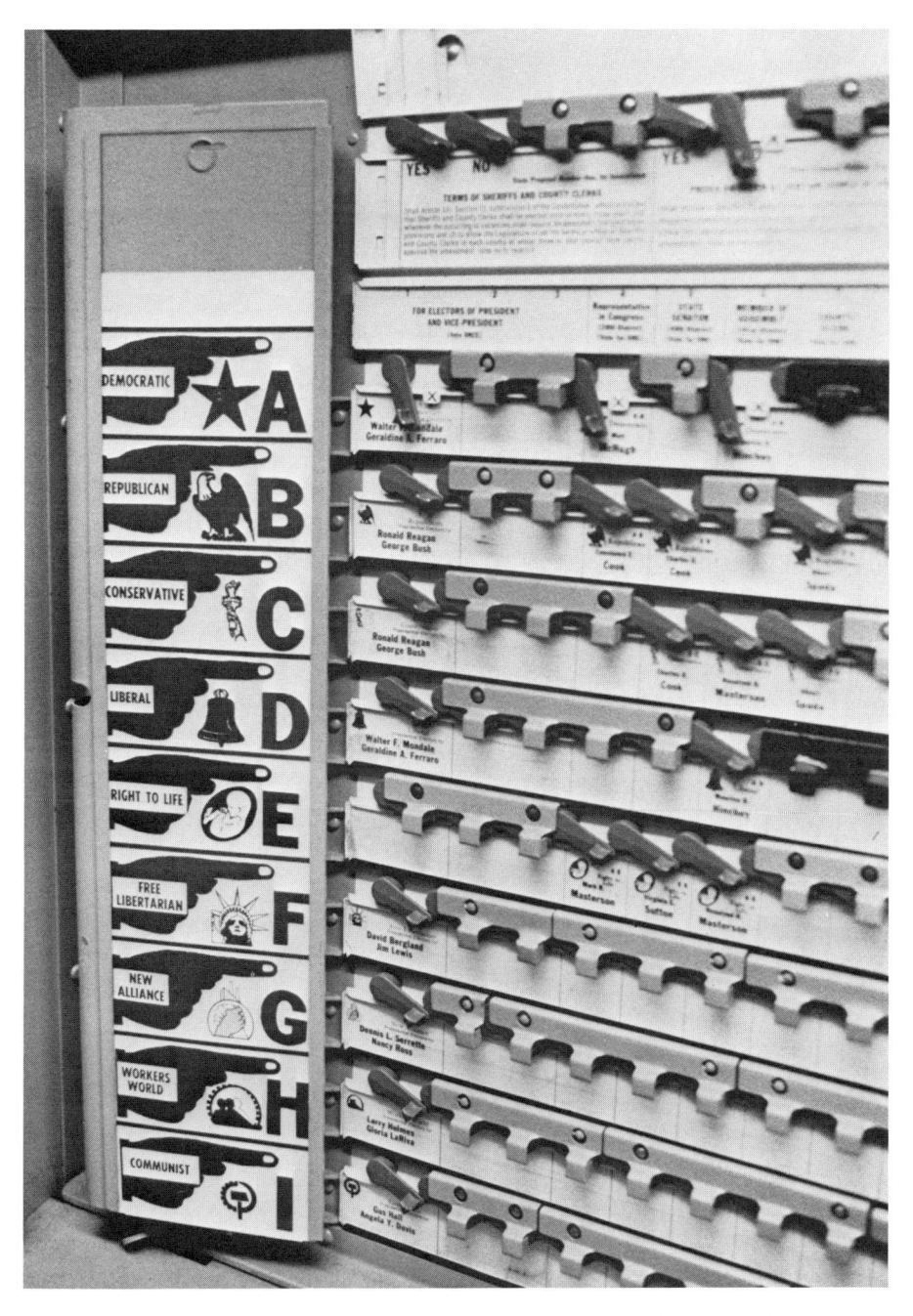

The voting booth—where would-be politicians meet their constituents. Every two years, the American people vote for a new Congress.

Who's Qualified To Run For Congress?

The United States Constitution lists the minimum qualifications that a congressional candidate must meet. These were decided on by the framers of the Constitution as a means to establish guidelines for selecting our country's leaders while maintaining the democratic nature of our government.

ACCORDING TO THE CONSTITUTION, A CANDIDATE MUST...

1. Be at least 25 years old (House); at least 30 years old (Senate).

2. Have been a citizen for at least seven years (House); a citizen for at least nine years (Senate).

3. Be a resident of the state he/she will represent.

4. Not hold any other federal office while serving in Congress.

Who's Qualified To Run For Congress?

To have a reasonable chance of being elected, however, a candidate must also meet a series of political qualifications. These are a little less obvious, and are often where would-be candidates run into difficulties.

THE POLITICAL REALITIES: A CANDIDATE MUST...

1. Be a resident of the congressional district he or she will represent.

2. Gain the support of an organized political party. For most candidates, this means running as a Democrat or a Republican.

3. Raise enough money to finance a lively election campaign.

4. Be able to "sell" himself or herself as a capable, qualified politician.

5. Project an image of being an intelligent, caring person who's in touch with the people.

canny old Chet Bannister out of the way, the race for the House of Representatives was wide open!

Dick had looked up the constitutional requirements. There was no doubt about it—he was qualified to run for a seat in the House. He was more than 25 years old, and he was an American citizen. He was also a resident of the state he would represent and he wasn't a convicted felon. Those were the only legal requirements.

Dick also knew there were unwritten political rules. For now, he decided not to worry about them. There were other things to do. He had to file "intent-to-run" papers. Then he had to build a campaign staff to help him compete in the June primary election. And that wasn't all. In order to become a full-time campaigner, he'd have to quit his job.

That was a scary thought. What if he lost? "I can always go back to real estate," he thought. "But if I win, I'll be my party's official candidate for the November general election. That's the final step on the road to Washington, D.C."

Finding Support, Raising Funds

Two weeks later, Dick answered the phone in his small, rented storefront office. He grinned as he listened to the excited voice on the other end of the line.

"Hey, Connie," he called as he put down the receiver. "That was Helen Vanderlip. She's worked out a half-price deal to get those flyers printed."

He watched his campaign manager as she taped a STOCKTON FOR CONGRESS banner to the window. Connie Mendoza was a veteran of district politics. It was a stroke of good fortune when she agreed to take a leave of absence from her newspaper to work for him. Connie had already run two political campaigns. Each time she'd brought in an upset winner.

Connie admired the banner for a moment, then went back to worrying about the bills piled up on her desk. It was still six weeks until the primary. That meant six weeks of rent payments and utility bills for their Main Street office. It meant paying for ads in the *Hillsboro*

Herald-Star and finding money to finance a last-minute mailing to district voters. She sighed and opened her books. The campaign also needed bumper stickers, campaign buttons, and a billboard on Oak Street. Then there were the radio and television spots. Those were really expensive.

"I'm guessing that you and your two opponents will spend half a million dollars on this primary election," Connie said.

Dick jotted some figures on a notepad. "My family's helped me raise $20,000, but that's our limit," he said. "The rest will have to come from individual donors and political action committees. It's too bad the law limits each contributor to a maximum of $1,000. My old boss would have kicked in at least $15,000."

Still, the news wasn't all bad, Dick decided. His program for redeveloping Turner Air Force Base was attracting plenty of attention. The air base closure was the most important issue of the campaign. Every mail delivery brought in checks from worried business people. But the staff was working against time. Connie often reminded him that she had to place printing orders and buy air time whether the money was in the bank or not.

Dick looked at the row of newly-installed telephones. The volunteers would be coming in soon to start their phone campaign. "They'll round up lots of $10 and $20 contributions," he told himself. To Connie, he said, "You and I will have to bring in some big donations. I want to raise enough money to plaster VOTE FOR STOCKTON posters all over the district. Right now, at least half the people I talk to have never heard of me."

The Primary Election

It was a week later and Dick was studying a tally sheet. Like most of the nation's 435 congressional districts, the Tenth District's population was close to 500,000. Of that number, the Republican and Democratic parties had each registered 90,000 voters. Another 20,000 voters were registered as independents or belonged to minor parties.

The registration numbers meant that 90,000 voters were eligible

Running for office means campaign slogans, TV ads, speeches, debates, buttons and T-shirts, bumper stickers and balloons. It's another form of advertising, and the product is the man or woman who wants to be elected—or reelected.

to take part in his party's primary. Of those, Dick guessed that only 45,000 would make it to the polls. Knowing that the three candidates would divide up the primary vote, Connie had written MAJORITY = 22,501 at the bottom of the sheet. The number reminded Dick that a majority win would guarantee him a place on the general election ballot.

He wasn't there yet. The polls showed that Dick was in second place, close behind the city's former mayor. He flexed his swollen right hand and thought about the days ahead. "I'm not sure my hand has enough shakes left in it," he thought.

Thanks to Connie, the candidate didn't have to shake every voter's hand. She had trained a group of eager "Volunteers for Stockton." These people were now contacting the 200-plus voters who lived in each of the district's 424 precincts. That was tough work. The volunteers had to sell Dick Stockton and his ideas to people who would rather be watching television.

Even though it was almost midnight, the office was still buzzing. Jeff Chen was editing a television spot and his assistant was writing press releases. Alicia Cohen was polishing tomorrow's speech, and the tireless Helen Vanderlip was balancing the campaign's finances for the third time that day. Tom Sweeney, the office manager, was filling the soft drink machine. Tom took care of the hundred-and-one details that no one else had time for.

The day had been typical. It started with a breakfast meeting, during which the staff made plans for the debate that night. After taping a television interview, Dick spent an hour calling local community leaders to ask for money. During lunch he'd spoken to the Rotary Club, and in the afternoon he'd dropped in on three neighborhood "Coffee with Stockton" meetings. Judith had joined him that evening for the debate with the other two candidates. People liked to see a candidate's spouse at campaign events.

Dick was getting less than six hours sleep a night, but the hard work was paying off. Thousands of people now knew who Dick Stockton was and what he stood for. Almost before he knew it, the sun was rising on the day of the primary. Had they done enough things right? Now it was up to the voters.

The Voters Decide

A tense crowd gathered at the campaign office that night. Dick sat quietly and chewed on a pencil. Nobody spoke.

The tension broke just before midnight. The final tally showed that Dick had beaten the ex-mayor by 12,000 votes. It was a landslide win! Dick's two opponents called to offer their support in the November general election.

The staff met the next day to plan the new campaign. The national committee sent word that it would support Dick with money and advisors. Dick smiled at the good news and handed out the results of a new poll. People were still worried about the closing of the air base. Without the base and the jobs it generated, the district faced hard times. The poll also revealed that voters were angry about Hillsboro's rising drug problem.

Dick made his decision. "We'll focus on redeveloping the air base as an industrial park," he said. "The buildings will be great for small, research-oriented companies."

"What about the crime-and-drugs issue?" Jeff asked.

"People with good jobs don't deal crack or steal cars," Dick responded. "'Vote Stockton for Jobs and Safe Streets.' How's that for a slogan?"

The days sped by. Dick spoke at factory gates, offices, and shopping malls. Everywhere he went, he told workers, "My opponent talks about saving the whales. I'll save your jobs!"

Connie set up a trip to Washington, where Dick visited the White House. The picture of his meeting with the president ran in the *Hillsboro Herald-Star*. The article under the photo reported that the president said, "I need Dick Stockton in Congress." The national party sent an all-pro basketball player and a film star to speak at Dick's rallies. More and more voters took notice.

Election day finally arrived. The Stockton campaign rented a ballroom for what the staff hoped would be a victory party. It was almost midnight when Dick walked into the noisy room. Channel 3 had just announced the results and the crowd was chanting, "STOCKTON! STOCKTON! STOCKTON!" The TV screens read:

> **For House of Representatives,
> 10th District
> Stockton—54 percent
> Hale—46 percent.**

"How do you feel, Congressman?" Dick's wife asked.

"I feel great!" Dick said. He walked to the microphone and thanked his supporters for their help. Then, as the cheering died down, he added, "I know I'm new at this job. But I'm a fast learner. The people of Hillsboro have put their trust in me and I won't let them down!"

2

A Lawmaker Needs Plenty Of Help

"A congressman's life can be summed up in one word," Dick Stockton wrote in his daily log. "That word is BUSY!"

Dick worked 12-hour days in the weeks between the election and the January swearing-in ceremony. Luckily, Connie Mendoza agreed to serve as his administrative assistant. Her job was to keep things running smoothly and arrange Dick's daily schedule. She also managed the flow of paperwork that came across his desk. Without Connie, Dick would soon have been hopelessly behind.

Together, Dick and Connie hired his staff. Along with his salary and other benefits, he was given an allowance to pay for up to 18 staff members. Dick interviewed people for his Washington office and the field office in Hillsboro. He hired four men and eight women, including Helen Vanderlip, Jeff Chen, and Alicia Cohen. Dick had come to depend on these talented, hard-working campaign workers.

Connie wanted to hire a computer operator named Sally Rich, but Dick said no. Rich was his wife's cousin, and hiring her would allow critics to accuse Dick of nepotism. Putting relatives on the payroll was against the law. More than that, Dick didn't want to be part of anything that might be unethical. He did hire Charlene Peskoff, an expert on planning industrial parks. He hadn't forgotten his promise to redevelop the closed Air Force base.

Congressmen must constantly be available to their constituents. After an individual is elected, it is important that he or she maintain a sincere interest in the people.

In early January, Dick moved into his offices in the nine-story Rayburn Office Building. Named for a famous Speaker of the House, the Rayburn was one of three office buildings used by the nation's 435 representatives. From his window Dick could see the white dome of the Capitol building a few hundred yards north across Independence Avenue. The office suite was divided into a large reception area, small offices for the staff, and larger offices for Connie and Dick.

A quick inspection tour convinced Dick that the Rayburn was almost a city in itself. It had committee hearing rooms, staff offices, a cafeteria, an underground garage, a gym and a swimming pool. "And

Roughly six percent of the seats in Congress are held by women Rep. Pat Schroeder (D.-Colo.) serves on the House Armed Services Committee.

that's not all," he told Connie. "There's also a recording studio. The technicians in the studio have a first-rate setup. As soon as I have my committee assignments," he decided, "I'll tape a video report for the folks back home."

Committee Assignments

Dick's study of Congress told him that the House did much of its work in committee. "I can't serve my constituents," he reminded himself, "if I get stuck on the wrong committees."

The House leadership chooses its members who will serve on the 22 standing committees. Each standing committee is further divided into subcommittees. A senior member of the majority party serves as the chairman. The majority party is always the party that holds the most seats in the House. Freshmen members can't hope to become chairmen, even of minor subcommittees. When Dick complained about the system, a congresswoman took him aside.

"You can't help your district by fighting the rules of the House," Harriet Douglas said. "Lots of people have tried and where are they today? They're back home, selling insurance!"

Dick accepted the advice. He didn't like the idea that he had to "go along to get along," but there wasn't any other choice. He could only hope that his party leaders would give him the committee assignments he wanted.

A party holds committee seats in proportion to its House membership. Because Dick's party was outnumbered 240 to 195, it received only 45 percent of the committee seats. That translated into nine seats on a 20-member committee.

Committee assignments were also based on seniority. The members who had been in the House the longest had first choice. In addition, members with special interests were given priority in their assignments. Lawmakers from farm states, for example, were first in line for seats on the Agriculture Committee.

Dick and Connie studied the committee lists. The Armed Services Committee looked interesting, but senior members had those seats locked up. In the end, Dick asked for two committees that reflected the needs of his district. "We'll go for the Small Business Committee and the Science, Space and Technology Committee," he told Connie.

Does It Pay to Serve in Congress?

Is Dick Stockton fairly paid for his work in Congress? Some political experts say "No." They worry that the salary and benefits aren't high enough to attract top-notch people. Many Americans, however, argue that politicians are overpaid. What do you think?

Category	Benefit
Salary	$99,500 (House); $101,400 (Senate)
Honoraria	House members are allowed to earn another $26,850 for making speeches and personal appearances. Senators are limited to $23,568.
Expenses	Members submit yearly claims for expenses. This allowance covers travel, telephone and FAX bills, newsletters, and other expenses.
Publications	The Government Printing Office provides many free materials for members to send to constituents.

Does It Pay to Serve in Congress?

Category	Benefit
Mailing	Free postage for official mail. This benefit is known as the franking privilege.
Offices	Members are given an office in Washington, D.C., plus field offices in their home states.
Staff	Members are given generous allowances for staff salaries. Senators who serve entire states receive two to three times more than Representatives.
Communications	Members are given unlimited long-distance telephone service. They pay a small fee to use government radio and television studios.
Pension	Any member who serves five years or more qualifies for a generous pension.
Other Benefits	Members receive free health care, legal advice, gym facilities, parking spaces and many other services.

Members of the same political party often meet to discuss the position of their party on different pieces of legislation, and to plan committee assignments.

"Both have over 40 members. I should be able to get one of my party's seats."

The party leaders approved Dick's choices. They liked young congressmen who didn't ask for impossible assignments. As soon as the appointments came through, Connie contacted the staff director who worked for each committee. The directors set up briefings that brought Dick up to date on committee business.

With the committee assignments came seats on several subcommittees. Dick was soon carrying a heavy load of paperwork with him when he left the office each night. When a friend asked him if he was having fun, Dick just laughed. "It's a great job. It would be even better if I had time to enjoy it," he said.

The Party Caucus

Dick jumped out of his chair and hurried to greet his guest. It wasn't every day that Willie Harrison visited a first-term congressman. Minority Leader Harrison was the third most powerful figure in the House. He ranked just behind the Speaker of the House and his main lieutenant, the Majority Leader.

Harrison took a seat and looked around the office. He seemed please to see Dick studying a stack of printed bills. "I see you're settling in nicely," he said in his Mississippi drawl.

It soon became clear that the Minority Leader was there to give Dick a quick lesson in House etiquette. The Speaker and the Majority Leader, Harrison said, try to steer their party's legislative program through the House. "This brings them into direct conflict with the President, who belongs to our party. My job," Harrison went on, "is to organize support for the President's program—and to defeat the majority party's strategies."

"Will I be working directly with you?" Dick asked. Harrison shook his head. He explained that Dick would have more contact with the Party Whip. "That colorful name," he said, "comes from 'whipper-in,' the member of a hunt who keeps the hounds from leaving the pack. I depend on the whip to know how the members are likely to vote. The whip also has to keep track of where the members are. I want to be sure my troops will be on hand when important bills come to the floor."

"What if I'm back in my district when a vote comes up?" Dick wondered.

"The whip will pair your vote with an absentee who's going to vote the opposite way," Harrison said. "In an emergency, we can ask the Air Force to fly you back here for the vote."

As Harrison left, he reminded Dick that he was expected to attend the party caucus. This was a meeting of the party's full House membership. During the caucus everyone has a chance to try to influence the party's stand on important bills. Dick understood the caucus was the best time to work out differences within the party. To do otherwise was to risk a public split in the party during a debate on the floor of the House.

Later, sitting alone in his office, Dick thought about the meeting.

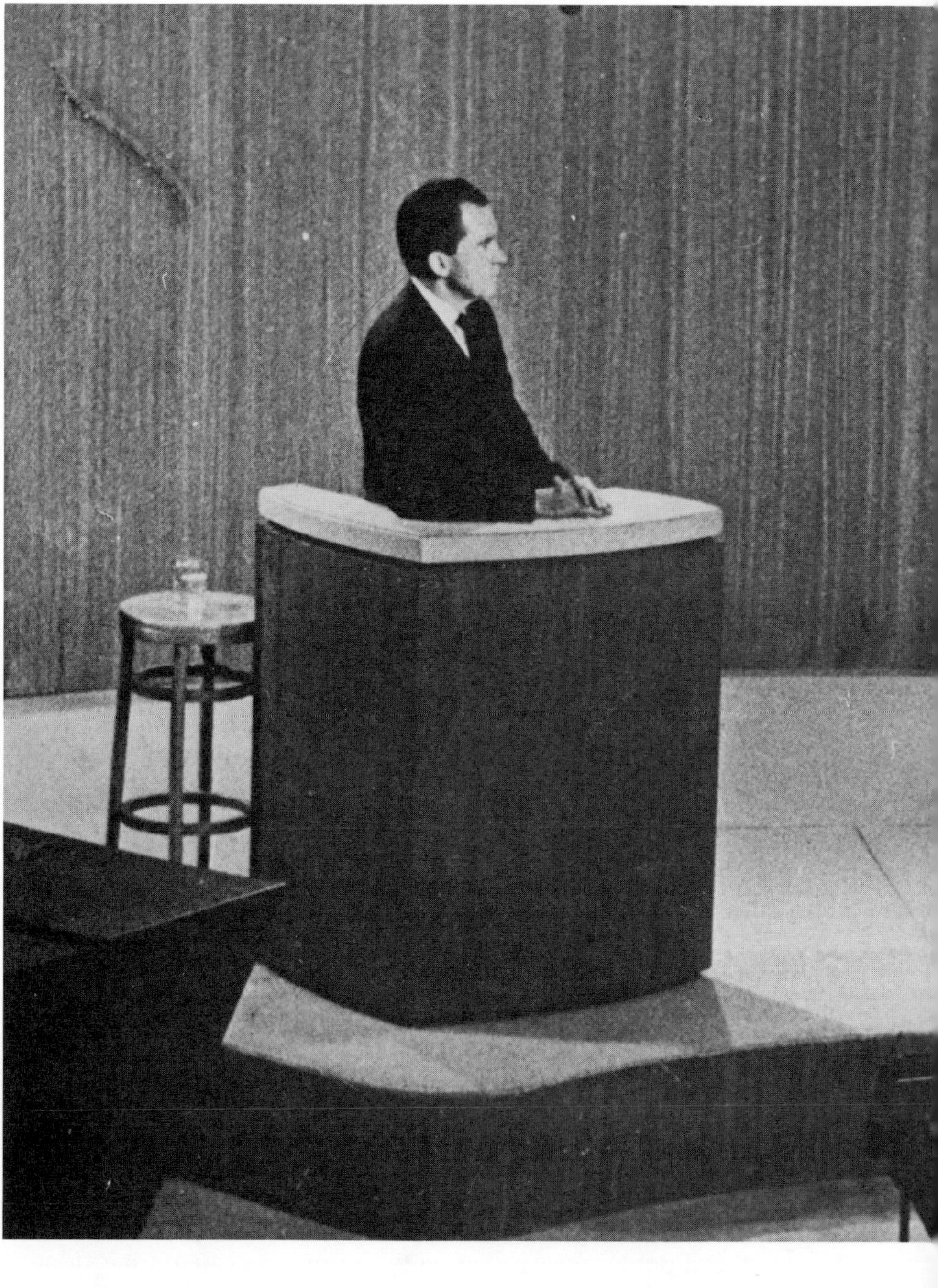

Former presidents Richard Nixon (left) and John F. Kennedy (right) both began their national political careers in the House of Representatives.

The Minority Leader had been friendly, but Dick sensed that Harrison could be tough if he had to be. There was no rule or law that could force Dick to vote with his party. But the party had ways of punishing those who voted with the opposition.

"Well, I'll cross that bridge when I come to it," Dick decided. "I'm not officially a congressman until I'm sworn in."

Long, Busy Workdays

The third of January was a red-letter day. With his wife and parents looking on, Dick raised his right hand at the Speaker's command. The new lawmaker then joined 434 other members in swearing to "support and defend the Constitution of the United States against all enemies."

At a family party that night, Dick explained the calendar to his father. "The Constitution requires that Congress assemble at least once a year," he said. "So, each term is broken into two annual sessions. This year we'll stay in session until August. After a 30-day break, we'll work until Christmas. Next year is an election year, so we'll try to adjourn by July 31. The members who are running for reelection need the time to campaign."

"You just got here!" Dick's mother protested. "You can't be thinking about a reelection campaign already."

"A two-year term zips by," Dick told her. "If I want to keep this job, I'll have to prove myself quickly. It was different a hundred years ago. Back then the sessions lasted only four or five months a year."

Like many of the members' wives and husbands, Judith Stockton decided not to move to Washington. She had a career of her own, and knew Dick would be home on many weekends. In order to stay in touch with his constituents, Dick planned regular Friday flights back to Hillsboro. After a weekend of politicking, he'd catch the Sunday night "redeye" flight to Washington.

Dick's workdays fell into a pattern. He met Connie for a working breakfast each morning to talk over the day's schedule. Then he put in a couple of hours in his office. This was a time for meeting constituents and reading the mail. If one of his committees was meeting, he studied the bills it was hearing.

Finding a quiet time to read and think was a problem. Connie screened his calls, but he spent what seemed like hours on the phone. Learning the job meant talking to party leaders, reporters, and important constituents. When he met his fellow lawmakers in the hallways, he pumped them for information about the inside workings of Congress. "You'll never last around here," a Texas congressman had told him, "if you don't know where the bodies are buried."

The House began its daily sessions at noon. One of the "inside tips" Dick picked up was that he didn't have to be on the floor all the time. When the roll call bell rang, however, he rushed to take his seat. Members who didn't show up to vote weren't doing their jobs. In mid-January he made his "maiden" speech in support of a water conservation law. But mostly he saved his energies for committee and constituent work.

3

You Can't Ignore Your Constituents

From the first day Dick knew he wanted to run for reelection. Carving out a strong record in Washington would help, but it wouldn't be enough. His constituents took it for granted that he would show up for committee hearings and floor debates. He had to come up with good answers to the question voters always ask their representatives: What have you done for us lately?

In order to find out what the people of Hillsboro wanted, Jeff Chen sent out questionnaires. As a member of Congress, Dick could mail them free of charge. His machine-printed signature took the place of a stamp. The first questionnaire asked for ideas about the redevelopment of Turner Air Force Base. Jeff also added questions on several "hot" issues. Should anti-drug money be spent to build new prisons? Do you support a federal ban on assault rifles? How can we improve our schools?

Dick often dropped into the computer room to watch Jeff work his magic. The young computer whiz had updated the mailing lists left by Congressman Bannister. By touching a few keys he was able to create address lists for special groups. If Dick wanted to ask senior citizens for their views on Social Security taxes, Jeff could furnish the address labels.

The Rayburn Building mail clerks picked up the outgoing mail and dropped off sacks of incoming mail. At first Dick tried to look at every letter that came in, but there weren't enough hours in the day. Harry Torcello took over the job. Harry sorted each day's mail and set aside the form letters and junk mail. Much of the mail demanded that Dick vote for or against a particular bill. Jeff prepared computerized letters that summed up Dick's position on these issues. Finding words to tell animal lovers that he wasn't going to vote for an animal rights amendment to the Constitution wasn't easy.

Each day Connie put three piles of mail on Dick's desk. The smallest was usually his personal mail. Dick answered the letters from family and friends with handwritten notes. The second contained a sampling of the day's interesting questions and pleas for help. Dick told his staff to give special attention to these letters. He sympathized with anyone who was caught up in the government's confusing rules and regulations.

The third stack contained what the office called "fan" mail and "hate" mail. Dick's "fans" wrote thank-you notes that made him feel good about the job he was doing. The "hate" mail was something else. Dick tried to laugh off the bad-tempered abuse, but it still upset him. Gun-lovers were especially outspoken. "Thanks to you sappy do-gooders," one man wrote, "innocent people are being machine-gunned in their beds by criminals."

The Field Office

In February Dick scheduled a trip back to Hillsboro to open his field office. He was going to make a speech and to greet a select group of his supporters. "They'll be checking to see if I'm puffed up with my own importance," Dick wrote to Judith.

Before Dick left the Capitol, Helen Vanderlip went over office finances with him. She reminded him that the government paid for only five round-trip flights a session. After that, Dick would have to buy the tickets out of his own pocket. They also looked at the books in which Helen kept track of office expenses.

"Opening a single field office is a good idea," she said. "You're entitled to two, but I don't think the budget will stretch that far. And taking an office in the post office building also makes sense. The taxpayers would growl if you rented an office in one of the expensive high-rise buildings."

What's in the Mailbag?

Wednesday, February 26, was a typical mail day in Dick Stockton's office. He received 250 pieces of mail that the staff divided into six general categories.

Category	Number of Letters	Description
Personal Mail	12	Letters from family and friends. Dick answers these letters himself.
"Fan" Mail	36	Letters from people who want Dick to know that they approve of his work or the way he voted on a bill. They receive a "thank-you" note.
"Hate" Mail	22	Letters from angry people who blame Dick for their personal problems or the country's problems. The staff tries to counter the anger with polite replies.

What's in the Mailbag?

Category	Number of Letters	Description
Requests for Information	45	People turn to their representative when they need information about government activities. If the staff can't answer the question, the letter is forwarded to the proper government agency.
Requests for Help	45	When people get tangled in government red tape, they write to their representative for aid. Dick and his staff advise the writers on how to solve their problems. They check back to see if further help is needed.
Demands For Action	90	Hotly contested bills bring letters in great numbers. Each writer wants Dick to vote a certain way on the bill. The staff keeps a tally of how this mail is running.

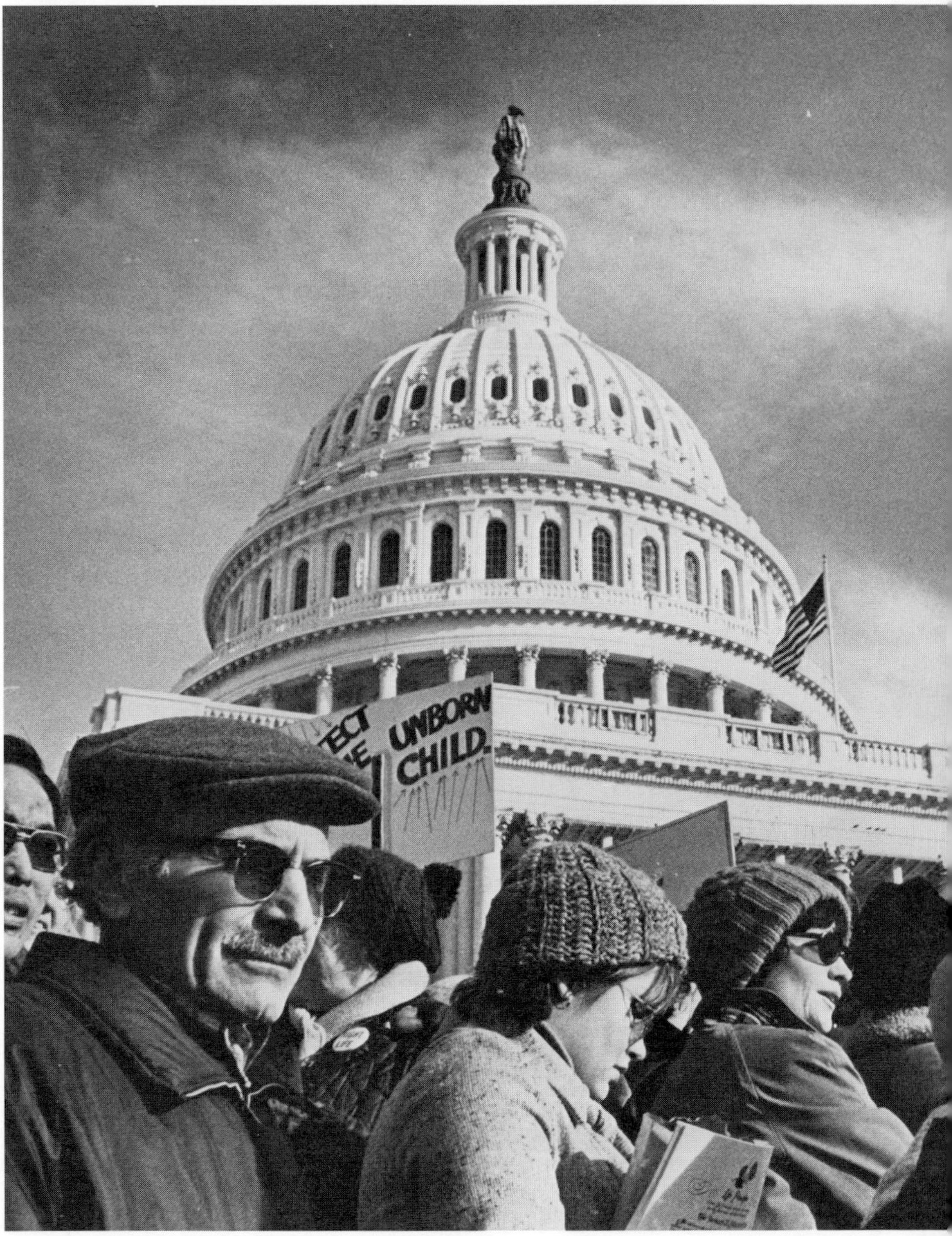
UNBORN
CHILD

An abortion protest rally at the Capitol building. Congressmen are the targets of many special interest groups who desire legislation that favors their cause.

"The post office building is a good central location," Dick agreed. "We need to be where people can find us." He looked over the columns of numbers. "Have we really spent all this money already? Well, hiring good staff people makes sense. DuPrez is doing a great job back there."

Dick talked to Jim DuPrez by phone almost every day. But the former schoolteacher was on his own when citizens came in with problems, questions, and complaints. He quickly learned how to put out fires before they flared out of control. With the help of a secretary, Jim also answered much of the field office mail. He was good at finding answers to all kinds of questions. The toughest ones were sent on to the Washington office.

When Dick and Judith walked into the field office on Saturday, they were greeted by cheers and applause. Colored banners gave the office a festive air. Hillsboro's new mayor rushed forward and shook Dick's hand as cameras flashed. Dick looked around and saw many of the city's most important business owners. Jim had turned the office opening into a political event.

"Where were the television cameras?" wondered Dick. "Wasn't Channel 3 covering the opening?" No, the Evening News crew wasn't there. For a moment Dick was annoyed, but then he smiled at his own sense of self-importance. "Watch out, you're beginning to think like a politician," he told himself. There were more important things happening in the world than the opening of Dick Stockton's field office.

Dick grabbed a sandwich from a tray. Soon he was deep in a debate with the mayor about the air base redevelopment.

An Office Full Of Visitors

Dick didn't have to fly back to the Tenth District to meet with all his constituents. Anyone from Hillsboro who visited Washington was likely to show up at his office. The visitors looked upon Dick as their congressman.

Congress was full of stories about members who ignored their home districts. Dick wasn't one of them. He instructed his staff in the "care and feeding" of constituents. Jeff Chen did his part by preparing a visitor's kit. The packet included maps, guide books, and a summary of Dick's work in Congress. For her part, Connie contacted Dick whenever visitors arrived. If he could, he'd slip out of a hearing or a floor debate to say a quick hello.

Some visitors simply wanted to shake Dick's hand. Others picked up tickets to the Visitor's Gallery. The gallery provided a bird's-eye view of the action on the floor of the House. Along with the visitor's kit, the staff also handed out passes for the special morning tour of the White House.

Connie's records showed that visitors took more than four hours a week of Dick's time. Most people were content with a quick tour of the office, but others demanded a few moments of conversation with the congressman. Noisy groups of children bombarded Dick with questions and asked for autographs. Another group of visitors came looking for assistance. They ranged from inventors with patent problems to students with research papers to write.

Members of the Hillsboro power structure received the red carpet treatment. They were the wealthy contributors, business owners, service club presidents, and union leaders he depended on for support. When President Betty Prentice of the Hillsboro School Board arrived, Dick took her to lunch in the Capitol cafeteria. Afterward, Dick invited her back to his private office to talk about federal aid for education.

Dick drew a hard line between visiting constituents and visiting lobbyists. "I suppose most lobbyists are honest, but they represent special interests," he told Connie. "I'm not going to end up in anyone's pocket. I'll talk to those who have information I need, but I won't take favors from them. Tell them that. Be polite, accept their research papers if they look useful, and explain my position on the issues. Let them know that I'm representing my district, not their special interests."

The Business Lobby

Connie stuck her head into Dick's office. "I remember what you said the other day," she said. "Should I cut off all lobbyists at the pass?"

Dick grinned at her. "No, the good guys get in," he said.

Connie knew what he meant. The economy in the Tenth District depended largely on three big corporations. The companies created jobs, paid taxes, and supported many of Hillsboro's smaller stores and businesses. It was vital that these large employers stay prosperous.

*The Capitol Building in Washington, D.C., where both the
Senate and the House of Representatives meet
twice a year to write new legislation.*

Dick kept in touch with the three companies. Thus, he wasn't surprised when President Mike Tarango of Tarango Steel flew to Washington to see him. Tarango had three items on his wish list.

"We're being badly hurt by imported Asian steel," he said.

"First, get us some limits on imported steel. Until we finish modernizing our plant, we can't compete with Asian prices. Second, try to convince the government to buy products made with American steel. We shouldn't be building bridges with imported steel. Finally, we need tax breaks to help pay for new equipment."

Dick knew that Tarango was handing him an almost impossible task. His one vote couldn't pass a bill without the support of the president and a majority in Congress. He said he understood the problem and promised to do his best.

His chance came when the House was debating a new tax bill. Dick took the floor and spoke about the problems of American steel companies. He proposed an amendment to limit imports and to give tax breaks to companies that modernized. The amendment was voted down, but Dick's speech made headlines in Hillsboro. Tarango phoned the next day to say thanks and to urge him to keep trying.

When Dick went home, he sometimes visited Tarango Steel, Greenwood Food Products, and Moritsu Lasers. Company officials gave him tours and loaded him down with statistics that would help him in his committee work. That was where he met the lobbyists for their industries. Because they were working for the same goals as he was, Dick put them on his Good Guy list. Along with accurate, up-to-date information, the lobbyists helped him when he drafted legislation. Bills had to be written in proper legal language, and Dick wasn't trained as a lawyer.

The payoff came when the three big companies held a luncheon for Dick. "We weren't sure about you when you won that election," Tarango said over coffee. "But you've already shown us more energy than Chet Bannister ever did. We hope you'll run for reelection next year."

4

Learning The Dimensions Of A New Job

Dick Stockton was taking a crash course in congressional politics. He soon found that his job did not start and stop at the office. It ruled his life almost every waking hour.

At least once a week, Dick ate lunch with Jeri Quincey. Ms. Quincey was chairwoman of the Small Business Committee to which Dick had been appointed. She and Dick shared an interest in Winston Churchill, the British wartime leader. When they weren't swapping Churchill stories, Ms. Quincey coached him in how to succeed at committee work.

After one lunch meeting, Dick threw out the draft of a bill he was writing. "It won't fly," he told Connie. "Jeri's convinced me that I could never get a gas tax bill through the Ways and Means Committee."

Another useful friendship developed on the handball court. There, Dick sweated out twice-weekly matches with Jameson Horace Tolliver. J.T. was chairman of Dick's second committee, the Science, Space and Technology Committee. After a match he liked to sit in the sauna with Dick to talk about the more serious game of politics.

One of J.T.'s "lectures" concerned committee chairmen. Until the 1970s, the senior member of the majority party was always picked as chairman. Younger members finally rebelled, and the committee leaders were now elected by the party caucuses. The change came about

Trying to make a bill become law is what members of Congress do. They want to enact legislation that they think is best for their districts, their constituents, and the country. Because people disagree over what government's proper role is, we have 535 men and women in Congress to debate it during every session.

How Does the Gover

- Can veto laws passed by Congress
- Influences Congress by shaping public opinion
- Proposes legislative program and yearly federal budget

- Can override President's veto with two-thirds majority
- Senate ratifies President's appointments and treaties
- Control of budget forces Executive Branch to compromise over policies and programs

Executive Branch
(President, Cabinet, and Executive Branch Agencies)

ENFORCES THE LAW

- Judicial review of Executive Branch actions
- Lifetime appointments minimize presidential influence

- Appoints federal judges
- Grants pardons and reprieves
- Decides on how vigorously to enforce court orders

Judicial Branch
(Supreme Court and other Federal Courts)

INTERPRETS THE LAW

...ment Stay in Balance?

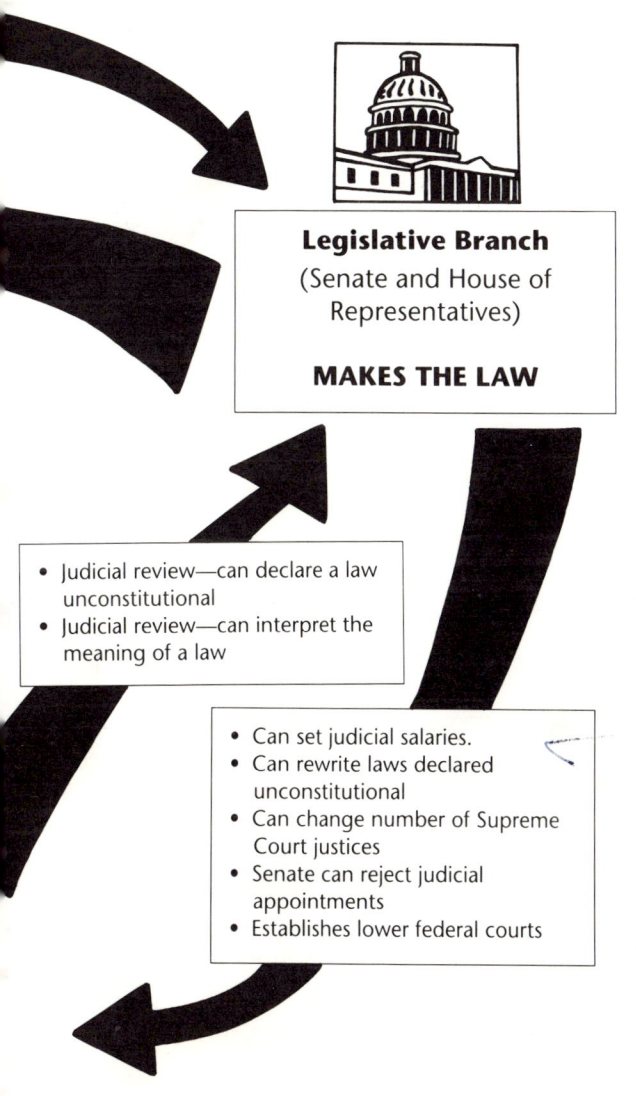

Legislative Branch
(Senate and House of Representatives)

MAKES THE LAW

- Judicial review—can declare a law unconstitutional
- Judicial review—can interpret the meaning of a law

- Can set judicial salaries.
- Can rewrite laws declared unconstitutional
- Can change number of Supreme Court justices
- Senate can reject judicial appointments
- Establishes lower federal courts

The Framers of the Constitution created three equal branches of government. Wisely, they designed the system in such a way that each branch "checks" the power of the other two. In this way, the federal government stays in balance and democracy is preserved. In this diagram, arrows represent the ways each branch checks the other two.

because of the power held by committee chairmen. They could make or break almost any piece of legislation sent to their committees.

Today, J.T. said, chairmen no longer kill bills by "shelving" them. Every bill must be sent to a subcommittee. But chairmen can—and do—send bills they don't like to hostile subcommittees. Even if the bill survives, a chairman can push the full committee into preparing an unfavorable report to the House.

At J.T.'s suggestion, Dick made friends with the committee staffs. These civil service employees are hired to do the committee's research and clerical work. They draft bills and amendments and plan the committee's public hearings. Staff members also helped Dick prepare questions to ask witnesses who testified before his committees.

The sharp questions helped Dick bring vital information to the committee's attention. They also helped him nail a few witnesses who were misstating the facts. One such exchange with a labor leader was broadcast on the evening network news. The folks back in Hillsboro will like that, J.T. observed.

"Members of Congress get the glory," Dick thought. "But we couldn't do our jobs without the help of our staffers."

Middle Of The Road

It was a Friday noon and Dick had just beaten J.T. in a close match. The two friends dragged themselves to the sauna and smiled wearily at each other.

"You're making progress," J.T. said. "I like your style, both on the handball court and in the hearing room. Are you sure you don't want to switch sides and join me in the majority party?"

"No way!" Dick laughed. "We're going to be the majority party, come the next election." On that note, he and J.T. headed for a late lunch in the House cafeteria.

Despite Dick's joking response, the exchange had touched a nerve. He knew that many issues that came to the floor of the House were decided along party lines. Democrats tended to support one set of interests and Republicans another. But Dick was elected to represent his district, not just his party. What if the party supported a clean air bill that would cripple Hillsboro's smokestack industries? What would happen if he voted against the party? Would its leaders support him when he needed votes for his redevelopment plan?

It's lucky, he decided, that party members don't all have exactly similar beliefs. Both parties divide into liberal and conservative wings. Generally, a liberal expects government to solve major social problems. Conservatives say that big government is inefficient and prefers to turn problems over to private individuals or companies. Thus, liberals would vote for a universal health care plan financed by government funds. Conservatives would agree on the need for improved health care, but they'd want to see the plan operated by private insurance companies.

Dick took a middle, moderate road. Moderates believe that government must play an active role in attacking problems. But, they add, government is often wasteful. Dick wanted the federal government to operate with the resources it already had. The huge national debt worried him.

That thought caused Dick to turn to J.T., who was enjoying a bowl of the cafeteria's famous bean soup. "I get at least a dozen letters a week that complain about costly 'pork-barrel' projects," he said. "Isn't it time for us to close down the pork barrel?"

J.T. looked at him sharply. "The pork barrel pays for federal projects in our home districts," he said. "It's a way to reward party loyalty. If you're not reliable, your party will see that your constituents don't receive much federal money. Speaker Sam Rayburn once said that congressmen must serve the needs of the other members as well as the needs of their constituents. Those who do not, he said, can never gain influence or power.

"Besides," J.T. concluded, "the pork barrel isn't all bad. Take your air base redevelopment plan, for example. Some folks might call that a pork barrel project."

"Hold on," Dick said. "We both know that the redevelopment won't cost the taxpayer anything. In fact, it will create jobs and generate taxes. That's not pork-barrel politics."

Meeting The President

Connie was waiting when Dick breezed into the office. "How was your breakfast with the president?" she asked excitedly.

Dick dropped into his chair and chuckled. "It was just a small

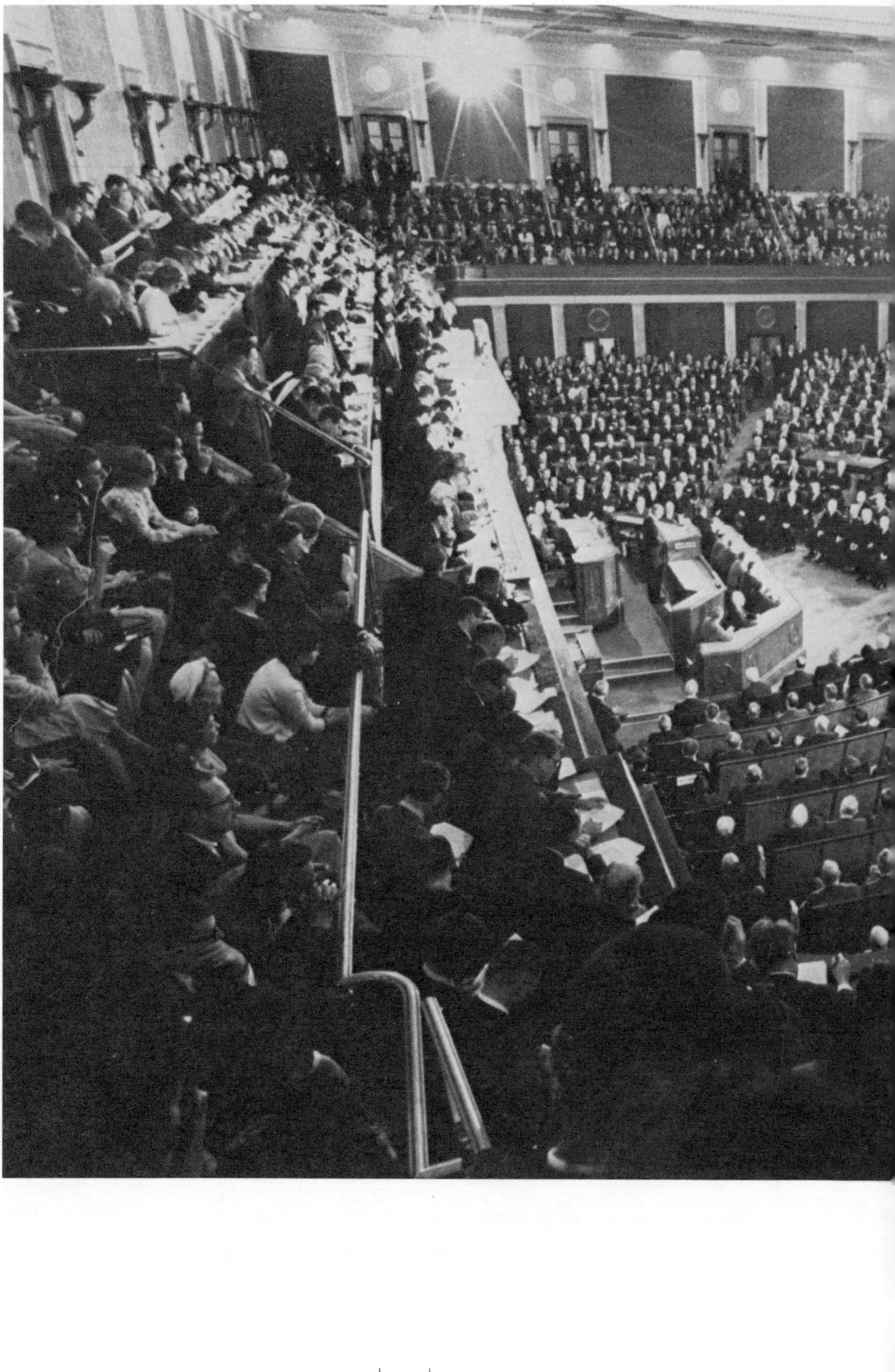

The House Chamber.

The President often meets with members of Congress in the Oval Office of the White House in order to influence legislation.

affair," he said. "Only me and fifty or so other first-term representatives. The White House does make a tasty cheese omelette, though."

Despite Dick's flip remarks, any contact with the president impressed him. After all, the Chief Executive was popular, and Dick generally agreed with his policies. Unfortunately, the opposition party ruled Congress. At the breakfast, the president had asked for the legislators' help in pushing his programs through Congress.

Later, the president described another problem. Over the years, he said, the legislative and executive branches had always competed for power. "Now," he complained, "Congress is in the driver's seat. We've got to restore the balance."

Dick had mixed feelings about the president's plea. The Framers of the Constitution had created three separate and equal branches of government. Under the system of checks and balances, no branch was supposed to dominate the other two. Congress had the power to appropriate money and pass laws, for example. Without funds, the president was powerless to put his policies into action. And even if he vetoed a bill, the House and Senate could still override it with a two-thirds majority vote.

At times, Congress felt overwhelmed by the president's power. It was the president who commanded the nation's armed forces. It was the president who supervised the Cabinet departments and their millions of civil service employees. It was the president who administered the federal government's trillion-dollar budget.

Just the week before, Dick had also seen the president use another weapon. In order to put pressure on Congress, the White House staff called a news conference. Television cameras carried the president's plea for support into almost every American home. Two days later, Congress was buried in tons of mail. Most of the letters favored the president's position.

Dick could vote against the president, but there was a price to pay if he did so. His constituents might forgive him for voting his conscience. But he still needed the cooperation of the executive branch if he wanted to get his redevelopment plan off the ground.

The Task Of Oversight

Dick came to Washington with the idea that he was there to write, study, and pass new laws. His on-the-job training taught him about the concerns of constituents. Ms. Quincey and J.T. soon introduced him to a third major duty.

The third duty was that of oversight. The American people depended on Congress to oversee the operations of the executive branch. The Science, Space and Technology Committee, for example, watched over the nation's space program. Was NASA conducting its space flights according to plans approved by Congress? Dick remembered the Challenger disaster as he questioned NASA officials about their safety program. "We won't lose another space shuttle if I can help it," he wrote in his log.

Ending programs that had outlived their purpose was a harder task.

Outside a rescue mission in downtown Albany, New York. Unemployment and homelessness are serious social problems tied closely to our economy. Year after year, Congress must approve a national budget to deal with these problems.

No agency would admit to Congress that it wasn't needed any longer. Dick spent many evenings pouring over the reports submitted by the agencies that reported to his two committees. When he had questions, he went to the experts on the committee staff for help.

As part of the budget process, each agency sent its department heads to testify before Congress. Dick found that most government officials were competent and hard-working. "The incompetent managers," he wrote to his wife, "are easy to spot." He guessed that they owed their jobs to political connections. Some agencies were called on to testify so regularly that they set up offices in the Capitol building. If Dick wanted information from the Department of Defense or the Department of Veterans Affairs, their liaison officials were easy to reach.

Dick's constituent work also brought him into contact with the independent regulatory agencies. These powerful agencies cooperated because they depended on Congress for their yearly budgets. When a constituent asked for help in renewing the license for a radio station, Dick contacted the Federal Communications Commission. Complaints about consumer fraud went to the Federal Trade Commission. Trucking, the environment, the stock markets, and many other areas of national life were all monitored by dozens of regulatory agencies.

His plans for redeveloping the air base led Dick to the Small Business Administration. The S.B.A. officials helped him refine and expand the project. But they couldn't launch it. That had to wait until Dick's plans were approved by Congress.

5

A Congressman's Work Is Never Done

Dick Stockton felt most like a congressman when he took his seat on the floor of the House. Committee hearings are important, he thought, and working for constituents will help me win reelection. But this is where they count the votes.

Each day seemed to bring a new experience. In early January Dick slipped a plastic card into a voting console and pushed a button. Above the Speaker's chair, his first vote flashed on a large panel. When he made his first speech, every word was printed in the *Congressional Record* the next morning. "I'd better be careful," he told Connie. "If I get careless, my words might come back to haunt me."

A training seminar introduced Dick to the rules of conduct used in the House. His debates with other members, for example, were restricted to polite verbal fencing. No matter how idiotic the opponent, he or she deserved respect. Dick learned to say, "the distinguished member from Texas," or "my able opponent from the great state of Oregon." J.T. cautioned him never to make personal attacks or to question the motives of his opponents. If Dick violated these unwritten rules, some of his fellow lawmakers would refuse to support the bills he sponsored.

The sound of a bell ringing in the Capitol sent Dick racing to the House chamber. Even if he was in a committee hearing, the bell took

Congressional hearings are held by committees to gather information that will help them draft new legislation, or modify existing laws.

priority. A quorum call told him that roll would be taken to see if enough members were present to conduct business.

He also learned three ways of casting his vote. When a roll call vote was taken he had to go on record as voting "yea" or "nay." That was why many lawmakers preferred voice votes or rising votes. On a voice vote, the Speaker listened to the volume of "yeas" and "nays" and selected the loudest. A rising vote called for the members to stand and be counted as "yeas" or "nays." Both of these methods allowed House members to vote without putting their names into the record.

Dick spent as many hours on the floor as he could spare. At times

A State of the Union address, when the president of the United States visits Capitol Hill to report on national matters.

he was one of only a dozen or so members present. Then Willie Harrison or some other well-known representative would rise to speak and the chamber would fill up as if by magic. Dick followed these speeches closely. He chose as models those members who prepared carefully and spoke directly to the point.

In late January the president strode into the House chamber to give his State of the Union address. The chamber was filled that night with senators and representatives, Supreme Court justices, and other high officials. Dick was spellbound by the speech and by the excitement of the moment. The thought of going back to a dull committee hearing the next day made him groan.

Making A Mark In Committee Work

Jeri Quincey caught up with Dick as he was walking away from a subcommittee hearing. "Nice work," she said. "I wish everyone came to the hearings as well prepared as you do."

Dick smiled his thanks for the compliment. He'd already decided that a freshman congressman had to make his mark in committee. On the floor of the House, he was just one of 435 members. In a subcommittee, however, he was sometimes the only member who showed up for a hearing. Regular attendance and the long hours of study he put in at night were paying off. He was gaining a reputation for no-nonsense questioning.

Early in the session, Dick called a meeting of his staff. "I can't become an expert on every national problem," he said. "I'll have to specialize in a few areas. What should they be?"

Connie pointed to the needs of the district. "I know you're interested in space," she said. "But Hillsboro's industries don't do any space-related work. I think you should stick to plant modernization and small business redevelopment."

Dick focused his reading on those areas. Before long, the other committee members were looking to him for advice. He also found that he excelled in the executive sessions that followed the public hearings. These closed meetings gave the members a chance to discuss issues and to reach compromises. When a debate was bogged down, Dick often stepped in and summed up the arguments for each side. His fair-minded summaries earned him added respect.

"The price of successful committee work is boredom," he wrote to Judith. "Some of these hearings go on forever. Everyone wants to testify and most of the witnesses repeat what someone else has said. For every useful nugget we dig out, we have to sift through a ton of worthless testimony."

As part of his learning process, Dick dropped in on committee hearings that promised extra fireworks. He walked into a moment of high drama the day he attended an Armed Forces committee hearing. Unlike his own quiet committee sessions, the room was packed with reporters and television cameras. "What's going on?" he whispered to a staffer.

"The president of HyperDent Industries is testifying," the staffer

How Hard Do the Members of Congress Work?

Computer whiz Jeff Chen tracked Dick Stockton through a typical week. The results shouldn't have surprised anyone, because Dick's 59.3-hour workweek is typical for the members of Congress.

Activity	Hours	Percentage Of Work Week
Attendance on the floor of the house	15.3	25.8
Legislative research and reading	7.2	12.1
Reading and answering mail	7.2	12.1
Committee hearings and meetings	5.1	8.6
Working on constituent problems	3.5	5.9

How Hard Do the Members of Congress Work?

Activity	Hours	Percentage Of Work Week
Meeting with contituents	4.4	7.4
Committee hearings and meetings	3.5	5.9
Writing chores—speeches and articles	2.7	4.6
Taking care of party business	2.4	4.0
Meeting lobbyists and special-interest groups	2.3	3.9
Media chores—interviews, taped speeches	2.1	3.5
Total	59.3	99.9

said. "He's trying to explain why his company's new battle tank can't shoot straight. By my count, Harriet Douglas has caught him in seven flat-out lies. Watch, she's ready to lower the boom on him right now."

Dick settled back to watch the veteran congresswoman at work. Before she's through, he thought, she's going to make sure the Army gets its money's worth from HyperDent. And if she ever runs for the Senate, the publicity generated by this hearing should be worth half a million votes.

A Heavy Load Of Casework

"The mail isn't so bad," Dick thought. "At least I can deal with that in my own good time. It's the phone that bothers me the most." He was in his office, trying to draft a private bill for a Hillsboro constituent. Just then, the phone rang again.

It wasn't Connie's fault. She had the staff well briefed and the secretaries handled most of the calls. They listened to problems, referred callers to the proper agencies, and noted requests for printed materials. Routinely, they added the soothing words, "I'll bring that to Congressman Stockton's attention."

Connie took calls that couldn't be handled by secretaries. She talked to White House and committee staffers and agency officials. But the Minority Leader, committee chairmen, and important constituents insisted on speaking to Dick. His call-waiting button seemed to flash almost constantly.

Dick hung up the phone and went back to the private bill. When federal agencies can't—or won't—solve a constituent's problem, lawmakers often introduce private bills. These bills usually benefit just one person, family, or business. The bill Dick was working on was one of thousands that pass through Congress each year. If his bill passed, Eduardo Sanchez's Salvadoran wife would soon be joining her husband in Hillsboro.

The Sanchez case was just one of hundreds of problems that Dick called his "casework." In a typical week, the office took on 200 cases of varying difficulty. Tax, immigration, and veterans' problems were the most common. The paperwork filled most of the notebooks that lined the office shelves.

With a sigh, Dick shoved his papers aside. Would the House pass

Some congressional hearings draw crowds of spectators and media because of their controversial nature. The Iran-Contra hearings in the late 1980s packed this hearing room daily.

his private bill and help the Sanchez family? It was easier when he could pick up the phone and call the head of an agency. That was how he'd helped Del Appleton get his new wheelchair. Del was a crippled Vietnam veteran. He had asked the local Veterans Hospital for a racing wheelchair so he could compete in marathons. When the request was denied, Del contacted Dick's office.

Dick had called the V.A. hospital director. "This is Congressman Stockton calling," he said. That had been enough. Federal employees know that Congress controls the yearly budget for their departments. Del had his new wheelchair a week later.

A Busy Schedule

Some of Dick's public appearances seemed a waste of time. Others left him feeling good about the work he was doing. His appearance at the dedication of the new Hillsboro Veterans Hospital was one of the good times. When Dick looked at the audience, Del Appleton was in the front row. Del spun around three times to show off the mobility of his new wheelchair.

Invitations to civic events arrived by the dozens. Everyone seemed to want Dick Stockton. On Hillsboro's Armed Forces Day, Dick rode the parade route in the back of an army jeep. He bought the season's first box of Girl Scout cookies and pinned badges on Hillsboro's newest Eagle Scouts. He spoke at a high school pep rally and fielded questions from first graders. Wherever he went, people treated him with uncommon respect.

"Don't let it go to your head," Judith told him. "It's not you they're applauding, it's your office. Seeing you makes Congress seem close enough to touch. Like it or not, you're a living, breathing symbol of the government of the United States."

When he was in Washington, Dick taped a five-minute radio talk every Thursday morning. Each program discussed a different topic. In his even-handed way, Dick described both sides of the issue and then explained his own position. Before long, all three local stations were carrying his "Reports to Hillsboro." Reporters and talk show hosts also contacted him. They found that Dick always had a quotable opinion they could use.

Dick's least-favorite civic activity was attending dinners. Making speeches wasn't the problem—he enjoyed that and knew he was a good speaker. It was the tasteless banquet dishes that bothered him.

"The Booster's Club is trying to poison me," he whispered to Judith at one banquet. "The proof is right here." He pointed to the plate of greasy fried chicken and canned peas.

"Hush, they'll hear you," Judith warned. "Dining on warmed-over chicken is the price of fame and glory, Congressman."

Award ceremonies also took up precious time on his weekends in the district. Plaques and badges and photos soon filled his office walls. He became an Honorary Volunteer Fireman. He was installed as a member of the Stevenson School PTA. Cameras clicked as he crowned Miss Hillsboro and rolled a game with a championship bowling team.

"That's enough civic duties for a while," he told Connie when he returned to the office on Monday. "Let's get on with the job of passing that redevelopment bill."

6

Only A Few Bills Survive To Become Laws

At first glance, the problem seemed simple enough. Turner Air Force Base was closing down. The closure would rob Hillsboro of hundreds of jobs. So, why not redevelop the unused land and buildings as an industrial park? The park would attract new industries, save jobs, and keep Hillsboro prosperous.

"That's what I came to Washington to do. I'm not going to let you down," Dick promised in his weekly radio talk.

The plan almost fell apart because of laws governing the closing of military bases. The land could not be sold unless the Department of Defense certified that it was surplus. To Dick's dismay, the Air Force wouldn't cooperate.

The answer, Dick decided, was to write a new law. The law would force the military to sell closed bases when asked to do so by the Small Business Administration. For its part, the SBA would have to declare that the sale was vital to the area's economy. Like most good solutions, it seemed both simple and direct.

Turning an idea into a bill, however, is neither simple nor direct. Using other bills as models, Dick wrote out a rough draft of his Base Redevelopment Act. After the lobbyist from Tarango Steel helped him polish it, Dick took the draft to the Office of Legislative Counsel. The experts there did more than put the draft into proper legal language. They also studied other laws and court cases that might lead the courts

Rep. Thomas Foley (D.-Wash.), Speaker of the House in 1990. The post of Speaker is traditionally given to the most influential member of the majority party in the House of Representatives.

to declare the bill unconstitutional once it was passed. Thanks to their research, Dick was able to make several changes that strengthened the bill.

After all that work, Dick thought, trumpets should blow when I introduce this thing. Instead, the process was about as dramatic as eating an apple. In January of his second year in Congress, Dick handed the Base Redevelopment Act directly to the Clerk of the House.

The Clerk numbered the bill as HR 234. The number meant only that it was the 234th bill introduced in the House that session. As a favor to Dick, Senator Leslie Rumsford introduced an identical bill in the upper house. There, the bill carried the number S 197. In the House, the parliamentarian referred the bill to the Small Business Committee and the clerk sent a copy to the printer. When Dick next saw his bill, it filled 24 printed pages and named him as its sponsor.

"That's the first step," Dick told his staff. "Now we have to nurse our baby through committee."

Pushing It Through

Dick hoped for swift action, but things seemed to move in slow motion. His bill was placed on the committee's calendar and referred to subcommittee. Congress was capable of passing a bill in a single day, but that rare event happened only in emergencies.

The subcommittee's chairman didn't like Dick's bill, but he did schedule hearings. He protested that he was doing so only as a courtesy to a committee member. That was okay with Dick, who had seen dozens of bills die without ever being heard. The committee staff began to line up witnesses from government agencies, the business world, and the military. Dick recruited a delegation of Hillsboro's leading citizens to testify for the bill. He also told Connie to alert network television.

The day of the hearings finally arrived. Instead of a crowded hearing room, Dick found only three subcommittee members present. Seven others had skipped the hearings, as had the television networks. The hearing room was empty except for the subcommittee, two staffers, three witnesses, and a stenotypist.

Despite the slow start, the work went smoothly. To everyone's surprise, General Scully showed up to say that the military could live with the bill. Someone in the White House must have twisted the general's arm, Dick thought. The officials from the Small Business Administration were equally encouraging. "And well they might be," Dick thought—his bill would give their agency more power.

The Hillsboro witnesses were the stars of the show. A Chamber of Commerce study clearly showed the damage the closure would do to the city. What won the subcommittee over, Dick saw, was the emphasis on redevelopment. Most cities that lose a military base fight to have it reopened, but Hillsboro was trying to find new and productive uses for the property.

The hearings lasted a day and a half. Afterward, the subcommittee members met in closed session to "mark up" the bill. They checked it line by line, changing words and sentences to meet minor objections that had arisen. Then the subcommittee voted to approve the revised bill and sent it to the full committee.

Even then the bill was still in danger. The committee could have set it aside or called for more hearings. To Dick's relief, the committee voted a favorable report without amendments. No one submitted a minority report opposing the bill. Even so, Dick wasn't sure the bill would reach the floor of the House. The Rules Committee was still standing in the way.

Action On The Floor

When the Base Redevelopment Act left the committee it was placed on a calendar. Now it was up to the Rules Committee to decide when—and if—the bill would be debated. The members of this powerful committee serve as the House's traffic cops. They keep business moving by pushing some bills ahead and holding others back. As J.T. put it, "The Rules Committee does more than direct traffic. It also digs graves."

The Stockton bill escaped burial. At Jeri Quincey's request the Rules Committee gave the bill an open rule. The open rule sets a time for debate and opens the bill to amendments. A hard-to-obtain closed rule would have forbidden amendments.

The House took up the Base Redevelopment Act on a rainy day in early April. A Rules Committee member read a resolution that called for the House to turn itself into a *Committee of the Whole*. The proce-

How Does a Bill Become a Law?

Each year about 20,000 bills are introduced in the House and Senate. Only about 2,000 survive. The long road is full of pitfalls, as the flow chart below reveals.

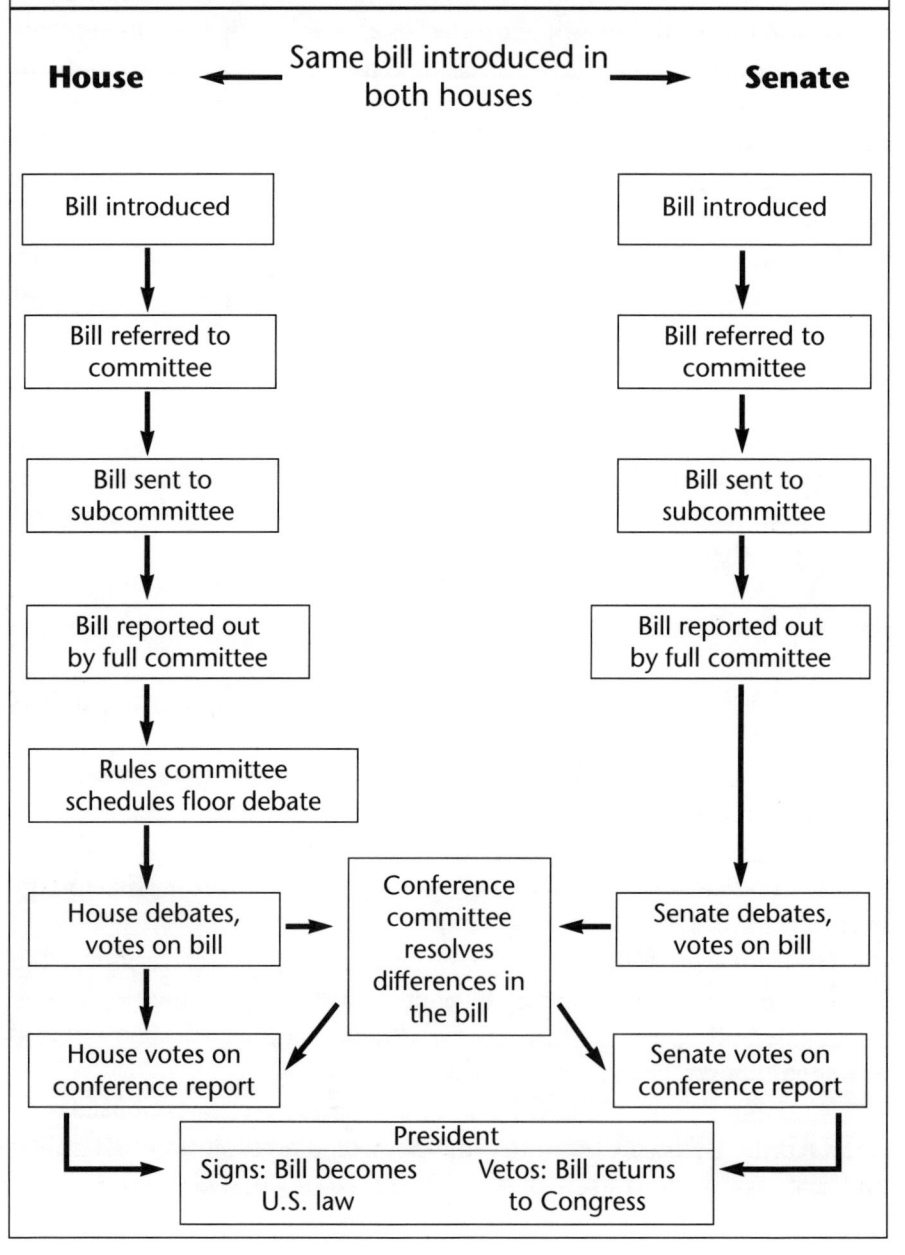

House ← Same bill introduced in both houses → **Senate**

House
- Bill introduced
- Bill referred to committee
- Bill sent to subcommittee
- Bill reported out by full committee
- Rules committee schedules floor debate
- House debates, votes on bill
- House votes on conference report

Senate
- Bill introduced
- Bill referred to committee
- Bill sent to subcommittee
- Bill reported out by full committee
- Senate debates, votes on bill
- Senate votes on conference report

Conference committee resolves differences in the bill

President
Signs: Bill becomes U.S. law
Vetos: Bill returns to Congress

dure streamlines debate, but the Committee of the Whole cannot pass a bill. Only the full House can do that. The Speaker set a time limit of one hour for the debate.

Dick rose to speak in support of his bill. The first speaker is usually a senior committee member, but Dick had asked for the chance. Alicia Cohen had helped him write an eloquent speech. When he finished, Dick had to laugh at his own conceit. He was speaking to a nearly-empty chamber.

The Small Business Committee managed the debate from tables near the front of the chamber. Dick looked at the list of members who were lined up to speak for his bill. He hoped it would be enough to escape the quicksand of party politics. The majority party didn't really dislike his bill. But as is often the case, the Speaker and his supporters just didn't want to give credit to the minority party for proposing it.

When the debate ended, the "second reading" began. Dick held his breath. Now was the time when members could try to change the bill. Many good bills had died under the weight of crippling amendments. Debate on each amendment was limited to ten minutes, five for each side. A few amendments were accepted, but the most damaging ones were defeated. The one that worried Dick the most failed by only ten votes. It would have scared away tenants by forcing them to "restore a base to its original condition" 30 days after the military gave notice that it needed the base again.

Finally, the chairman of the Committee of the Whole called for a voice vote. To Dick's immense pleasure the chorus of "ayes" clearly outweighed the "nays." That was a signal for the House to "rise." No longer a Committee of the Whole, it could now vote to adopt the bill as reported.

An opponent demanded a quorum call. The bells brought members hurrying in and the count soon passed 218. With a majority present, the House voted first on the amendments. Then it voted on the bill itself. Both passed, 268 to 92.

The Bill Goes To The President

Dick had won a battle, but not the war. The days were flying by and the bill was stalled in the Senate. He appealed to Senator

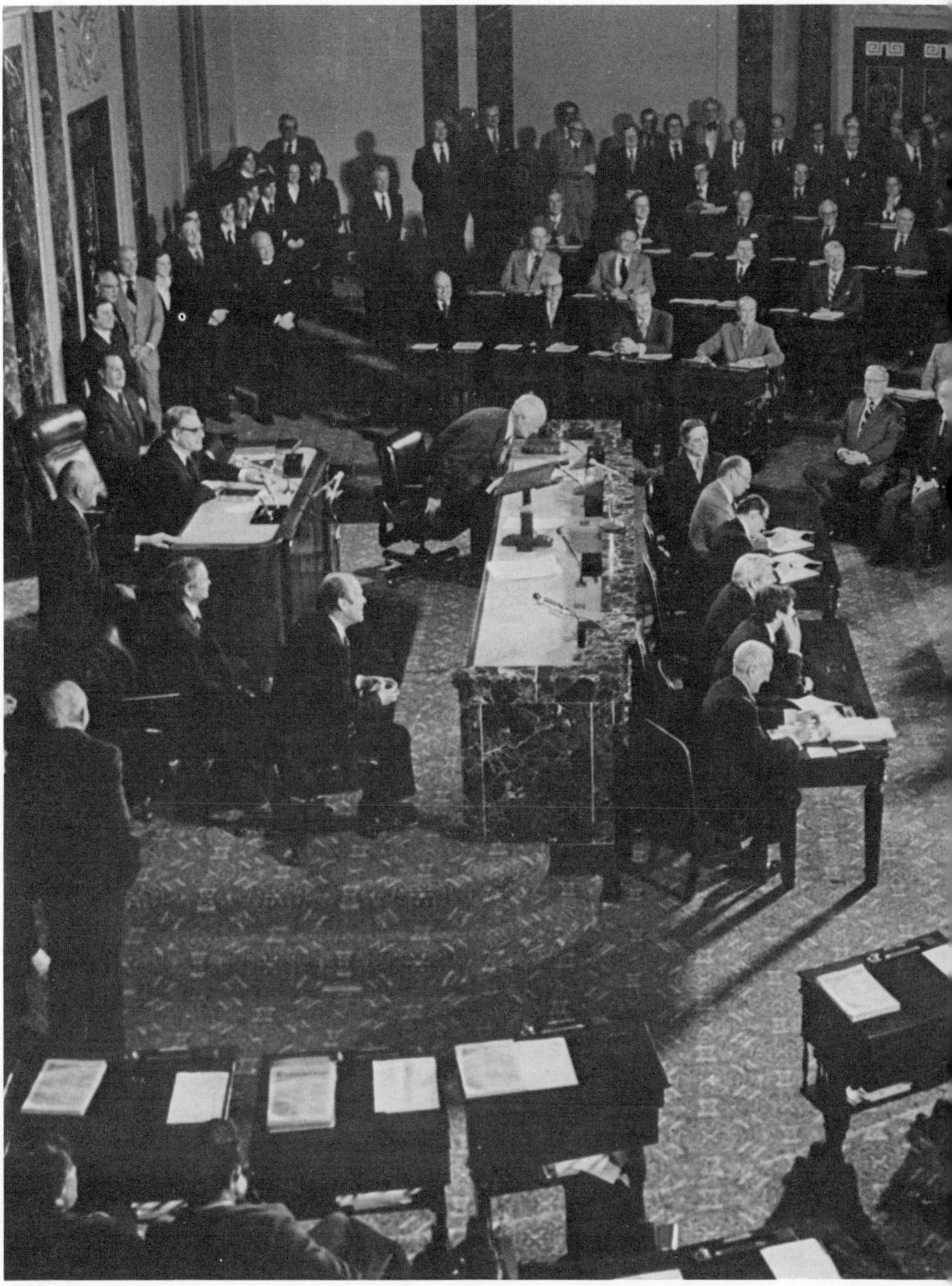

*The Senate, traditionally presided over by the
Vice President of the United States.*

Rumsford, who speeded things up by doing some political "horsetrading." A week later, the Senate Small Business Committee scheduled hearings.

The committee issued a favorable report on the bill in mid-June. Without a Rules Committee to delay action Senate leaders quickly scheduled the bill for debate. Dick wanted the bill signed into law before Congress recessed in July. If the bill missed that deadline, it would probably be lost in the rush to campaign for the fall election. A bill that isn't passed before the term ends in December must be introduced all over again in the next session.

Dick and Connie watched from the gallery on the day the Senate debated his bill. Unlike the House's padded benches, senators sat at small wooden desks. The senators can have their desks, he thought, but I do envy their six-year terms. That's enough time to really get comfortable in the job.

The Senate prides itself on never setting a time limit on its debates. If senators can't defeat a bill, they can try to talk it to death with a filibuster. "Rumsford doesn't expect a filibuster," Dick whispered to Connie. "I hope he's right."

Despite Dick's worries, the bill passed easily, 67-21. Thanks to several amendments, however, each house had created a different version of the bill. To solve that problem, the two bills were sent to a conference committee. There, leading members of each house met to iron out the differences.

No further amendments were allowed when the conference committee reported its compromise bill. Both the House of Representatives and the Senate voted for the conference report. The bill was then printed on parchment paper and signed by the Speaker of the House and the President of the Senate. Then it was sent to the President of the United States.

The president had several choices. If he liked the bill, he could sign it. Even if he didn't sign, as long as Congress was still in session the bill would become law in ten days. If he disliked the bill he had to veto it and send it back to Congress. In that case, only a two-thirds vote of both houses could override the veto and make the bill a law. Finally, if Congress adjourned within the ten-day period, the president could "pocket veto" the bill by ignoring it.

Because the bill was a victory for his party, the president never thought about using the veto. In early July Dick was invited to the Oval Office to watch the president sign the bill into law. After scrawling his signature, the president handed a souvenir pen to Dick. "Keep up the good work," he said.

7

The Struggle To Be An Honest Politician

As J.T. stripped off his handball gloves he said, "I had an interesting offer today. A lobbyist offered to set up a political action committee just for me. The P.A.C. is ready to funnel a cool $100,000 into my reelection campaign. All he wanted in return was a little help with the Justice Department. It seems the examiners are zeroing in on a savings and loan that's made some careless investments."

"I bet he didn't mention how much that help would cost the taxpayers, did he?" Dick said. "What are you going to do?"

"I threw the guy out of my office," J.T. said. "But not all ethical questions are that easy to resolve."

Dick sighed. "I know I'm here to take care of my 500,000 constituents. At the same time I want to make sure the U.S. Government manages its affairs honestly and efficiently. Those goals keep running into each other. I voted against a cut in social security taxes the other day and that upset a lot of people in my district. Don't they know the budget's in the red and Uncle Sam needs the money? Well, I can take that kind of heat because I know I'm doing the right thing."

"That's the problem," Dick thought. "That statement sounds good, but I don't always know what's right." The Party Whip had come by this morning to tell him his vote was needed to pass a strong defense budget. The party's important, Dick agreed, but sometimes its policies

Voters who want to influence the men and women in Congress often start petition drives to demonstrate support for (or opposition to) legislation on every issue imaginable.

ran counter to his own best judgment. Hillsboro, for example, needed federal money to help finance his redevelopment plan. Should he vote for one less Stealth bomber so Hillsboro could have more jobs?

"Let's turn it around," J.T. said, interrupting his thoughts. "Would you have accepted that $100,000?"

"That's easy," Dick shot back. "I'd have said, 'Thanks, but no thanks.' First, it's against the law. Second, if I accept, the lobbyist will expect me to do his dirty work. If I do that, I'll be selling out."

Dick felt comfortable with that statement. Honest politicians don't sell their votes. They don't use campaign money to pay for personal expenses. They don't vote to help companies in which they own an interest. But what about the "grey areas" where right and wrong are hard to tell apart? Is it wrong for a congressman to accept small favors from lobbyists?

"So far, so good," J.T. replied. "Now, what if this lobbyist offers you the use of the company plane for your vacation?"

Was J.T. reading his mind? Dick knew that some lawmakers accepted "favors" of that type. They had to answer to their own consciences, he decided. He wasn't going to accept any unethical offers. To prove it, he'd already made a public statement of his finances. The voters could see that he wasn't getting rich in this job.

"I may not be reelected," he told J.T., "but I'll lose with a clear conscience. I'm going to be as 'clean as a hound's tooth.'"

Raising Money For Reelection

Ethical questions were on Dick's mind because his two-year term was coming to an end. Like every other member of the House, he was up for reelection. The Constitution gave House members short terms so they would always be subject to the will of the people. What the men who wrote the Constitution couldn't have imagined was the cost of modern campaigning.

Connie took a leave of absence to run Dick's reelection campaign. She told him that the average House race would cost close to a million dollars. Over a two-year period that worked out to around $1,300 a day! The very wealthy could pay the costs out of their pockets, but Dick wasn't one of them. He would have to depend on campaign contributions.

Many people in Congress take trips or "junkets" to discuss trade between foreign countries and the United States. Congressmen have also gone to observe free elections in such countries as Poland and Nicaragua.

    The constant need for money raised further ethical questions. Tarango Steel was ready to help any way it could, Connie said. In return Mike Tarango wanted Dick to push harder for limits on imported steel. Dick wondered if he should agree. Quotas on imported steel would help Tarango, and that would help his district. The price of steel would rise, however—and steel goes into many of the goods used by the American people. More expensive steel means costlier autos, washing machines, and soup cans. Was that fair?
    Strict campaign funding laws made some of his decisions easier.

How Does Someone Become a Citizen Activist?

Many Americans pass up the opportunity of influencing government policy because they think no one listens. That may be true in a dictatorship, but a democracy's politicians must listen. If they don't, they'll lose their jobs at the next election. Here are some ways you can take an active role in government.

Activism Level	What Activists Do
Level 1: Listen and Learn	Activists stay tuned in to local, state, and national affairs. They follow the news in the media and discuss political affairs with their families and friends. They never miss a chance to vote.
Level 2: Take a Stand	Well-informed activists stick up for their political and social beliefs. They share their beliefs with others, but they try to understand opposing viewpoints as well. They vote in elections and try to persuade others to vote for their candidates and causes.
Level 3: Speak Up in Public Forums	A committed activist attends meetings and speaks out on the issues. The meetings can be local (school board or city council), state (an air-quality hearing), or national (a congressman's open forum).

How Does Someone Become a Citizen Activist?

Activism Level	What Activists Do
Level 4: Join an Activist Group	More determined activists join like-minded people and form special interest groups. Membership usually means that you're willing to pay dues, attend meetings, join protest marches, write letters to public officials, and give freely of your time and energy.
Level 5: Run for Public Office	The ultimate activist takes the final step and runs for public office. This is a major commitment of time, energy, and (sometimes) money. A successful election campaign puts you in a position to pass laws, set policies, and serve your fellow citizens.

He was allowed only one campaign committee. Connie had to account to the Federal Election Commission for all loans, contributions, and spending of more than $200. Violations brought penalties and bad publicity. Dick ordered Connie to play it straight. He liked headlines such as "Stockton Saves Jobs." He could do without "Stockton Violates Campaign Laws."

The law also restricted the amount of money that his supporters could contribute. Individuals were limited to gifts of $1,000 for the primary and another $1,000 for the general election. Corporations and labor unions were forbidden to make contributions, but the law had a loophole. Any special interest group could set up a *political action committee*, or P.A.C. P.A.C.s were allowed to collect money from their members (including corporations and labor unions) to give to candidates. Each P.A.C. was limited to $5,000 per candidate in any one election.

Dick smiled when he looked at his financial report. When he was an unknown candidate, he'd been forced to go into debt to help pay for his campaign. Now, as a popular incumbent, the money was rolling in. It's no wonder, he realized, that 90 percent of all congressional incumbents are returned to office.

Junkets, Gifts, Honorariums

Dick flew back to the district for a weekend of open forums set up by Connie and Jim DuPrez. He spoke to groups that ranged from alert senior citizens to angry steelworkers. After giving his set speech, he fielded questions from the audience. The "junket" issue surfaced at one of these forums.

"You say you're in Washington to serve the people," a young woman yelled. "How can you do that if you're taking junkets at the taxpayer's expense?"

A recent public service television program had reported on lawmakers who go on "fact-finding missions." To viewers, the trips looked a lot like free vacations. Dick also remembered the times when he couldn't contact his fellow House members. As often as not, a secretary would tell him that her boss was "fact-finding" in London or Tokyo.

Dick assured his audience that he hadn't taken any junkets. "If the

President asks me to represent him abroad," he added, "I'll certainly do so. And if meeting foreign leaders on their home ground helps me serve you better, I'll do that, too. Some members do abuse the privilege, but there's an easy answer for that. Vote them out of office!"

The mail sometimes brought another ethical problem. What should a politician do about the gifts that arrived almost daily? Small gifts of food and handicrafts didn't worry anyone. The staff sent a thank-you note to the donor and gave the gifts to shelters for the homeless. If the value of the gift exceeded $25, however, Helen Vanderlip mailed it back to the sender. With the package went a form letter explaining that government employees cannot accept valuable presents.

With his checkbook almost empty, Dick did accept several honorariums. These are the payments lawmakers receive for speaking at conventions, seminars, and graduations. Typical was the day Dick flew to New York to speak to the Children's Book Council. In return, the council paid his airfare and handed him a check for $1,000.

The laws were clear on these payments, Dick told his audience. "I'm allowed to make up to $26,850 a year in this way. The rules do set limits on how much I can accept for any one appearance." Then he drew a laugh by adding, "But freshman legislators aren't in great demand. Most of the people who invite me to speak think I should pay them for the privilege."

Getting Out The Word

Dick chuckled when he picked up one of Jeff Chen's reports. Jeff had drawn a hangman's noose in the margin. Hanging from the noose was a body labeled "Voters of Hillsboro."

"What's this all about?" Dick asked his computer expert.

"I'm ready to hang our fine constituents," Jeff said. "I send out questionnaires and only a few people sent them back."

That was a problem, Dick knew. Their first questionnaire had gathered a good response. After that, the number of returns went down rapidly. In a good month they were now getting back only one in seven. He told Jeff to cancel the questionnaires until a hot issue came along. In the meantime they'd concentrate on sending newsletters. The election was near and he needed to remind people that Congressman Stockton was doing great things for them.

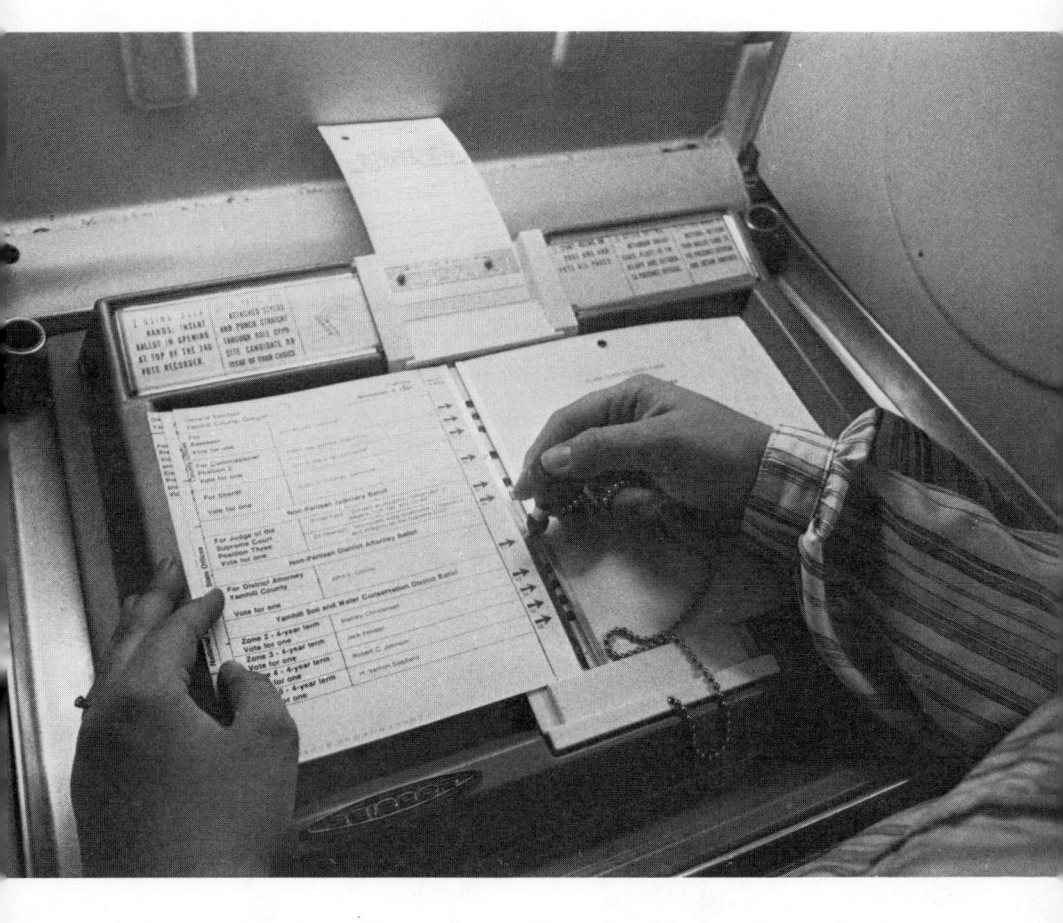

A Congressman faces his toughest critics when it's time for an election. Here, a voter looks at a ballot.

The newsletters were mailed free of charge thanks to Dick's franking privilege. The custom of giving free mail service to each member of Congress was older than the Constitution. The handful of letters that were franked in the 1770s had now grown to millions of pieces of mail a year. In fact, the post office had given up on the task of counting each item. Mail clerks weighed a few sacks and multiplied their average weight by the number of sacks. Congress paid the costs from its own budget.

The volume of franked mail zooms upward during election years. By law members are forbidden to use their franking privilege to mail campaign materials. But a newsletter doesn't have to say VOTE FOR STOCKTON to be a political message. To politicians running hard for reelection, anything that puts their names in the voters' hands is helpful.

Jeff and Alicia made sure that the mailings made a good impression. Their four-page newsletters featured sharp photos and punchy copy. They pulled "fan" letters out of the file and ran them as proof of Dick's service to his constituents. Another issue featured the story of the passage of the Base Redevelopment Act. The picture of the president shaking Dick's hand after the bill was signed into law almost filled the front page.

Out in Hillsboro, Connie was preparing campaign mailings and television spots. As the law required, she kept all the costs separate from the office budget. Dick watched his campaign fund grow and crossed his fingers. So far, the opposition hadn't found a candidate to run against him. His reelection prospects looked almost too good to be true.

8

The Race For Reelection

"Why didn't someone warn me this was going to happen?" Dick glared at his staff and waved a copy of the *Hillsboro Herald-Star* at them. No one met his eyes. The headline said it all: "Sports Hero Jumps Into Race Against Stockton."

The campaign had been going too well, everyone agreed. Dick had tended to business at the Capitol while Connie and Jim planned strategy back in the Tenth District. The campaign fund was fat and no one had challenged Dick in his party's primary. Now, almost at the last minute, the opposing party had talked Tank Colorado into joining the race.

Well, actors and generals run for President, Dick thought. Who's to say that football players can't run for Congress? The problem came down to name recognition. Even now, after almost two years, many Hillsboro residents couldn't name their congressman. But everyone knew Tank Colorado—the former pro fullback was a local legend. Having a well-known name was the first long step to winning an election.

Jeff Chen tried to inject a note of cheer into the gloomy meeting. "Hey," he said, "at least Tank's last name isn't Kennedy or Eisenhower. We're not up against a famous family or an experienced politician here. Just wait 'til you get ol' Tank hooked up in a debate. You'll make him look as though he played too many games without his helmet."

Dick smiled and remembered to count his blessings. His redevel-

A reapportionment map of New York City, showing how congressional districts are drawn up every ten years. The number of seats that each state occupies in the House of Representatives can change depending upon the most recent population count.

How Is a Political Party Organized?

A political party can be defined as a group of people who join forces to elect candidates who share their social, economic, and political views. A successful party organization begins in local neighborhoods and extends upward to the national scene. In simplified form, the structure looks something like this

Level	Tasks
National Committee	Writes the party's national platform. Organizes the national convention at which the party chooses its presidential and vice-presidential candidates. Aids party candidates who are running for Congress and for state offices. Carries on extensive fundraising operations.
State Central Committee	Supervises the selection of candidates for state offices. Organizes the state convention. Distributes political favors to faithful party members. Raises campaign funds. Coordinates the work of city and county committees.

How Is a Political Party Organized?

Level	Task
City and County Committees	Coordinate county political activities and election campaigns. Distribute local political favors. Raise money for local election campaigns. Send delegates to state and national conventions.
Precinct Workers	Work for party candidates at grassroots level. Conduct get-out-and-vote activities. Raise money for the party. Send workers to watch the polling places on election day.
Party Members	Support party's candidates with votes and contributions of time and money. Most will vote for any candidate the party nominates. Others vote the party ticket only if they believe in the party's platform and its candidates.

opment plan had been signed into law, and he hadn't been hit by a redistricting problem. Every time a state gained or lost seats following a national census, the legislative districts had to be redrawn. If that ever happened, the majority party in the state legislature would probably *gerrymander* his Hillsboro district.

Gerrymandering is the game of setting up "safe" districts for the majority party. But voters don't live in neatly-shaped Republican or Democratic areas. In order to create safe seats for its own members, the legislative majority draws weirdly-shaped districts. As a result, opposition lawmakers are often pushed into new districts where their party is outnumbered. Until the state designed new districts, however, Dick's party was still the majority party in the Hillsboro district.

"Well, let's hope Jeff's right," Dick said at last. "We'll go head-to-head with Tank Colorado. Put out a press release that says I welcome him to the race. Say that I'm ready to debate him anytime and anywhere."

Running On His Record

When Congress adjourned in early August, Dick flew back to Hillsboro. To his surprise, a cheering crowd was waiting at the airport. The high school band struck up a fight song and the mayor led him to a microphone.

Connie slipped in beside him and put a pack of 3x5 cards in his hand. "The campaign has begun," she whispered.

Dick saw that the cards outlined the basic speech he and the staff had worked on earlier. Two years ago he would have been terrified. Now he felt energized and happy.

He told his listeners that he was proud to have represented them in Washington. He assured them that he was enjoying his job and hoped to keep it. "With your help," he finished, "the Stockton-Rumsford Base Redevelopment Act has become a reality. This much-needed bill means jobs and prosperity for Hillsboro."

Running as an incumbent was a great advantage. In his secret thoughts Dick was already dreaming of the day when he'd be a six-term congressman. With seniority came committee chairmanships and a stronger voice at party caucuses. The added influence would give him a chance to do more for his constituents. It wasn't any wonder that the voters seldom replaced a veteran legislator with a political newcomer.

Everywhere Dick went people greeted him with friendly smiles. Their support made it easy to deal with hecklers.

"You jerk!" one red-faced man shouted. "You say you're for the people, but you voted against reducing Social Security taxes."

Because he felt confident in his voting record, Dick welcomed those challenges. He explained the problem of America's huge national debt. "Do you want to saddle your children with debt so you can have a few more bucks now?" he demanded.

The debates with Tank Colorado were the highpoints of the campaign. Crowds filled the civic auditorium and thousands more watched on television. The first debate was a draw, but Dick clearly won the next two. He discovered that his opponent was lost once he strayed from his prepared notes. Coolly, Dick raised questions that centered on technical aspects of the redevelopment plan and foreign policy. The low-key attack left Tank looking confused and unsure of himself.

The Results Come In

On election night, the staff rented the same ballroom they'd used two years earlier. "There is a difference," Dick thought. "Now there's more of everything—more banners, more people, more noise. I hope there'll also be more votes."

Dick needn't have worried. The early returns gave him a lead that increased with every precinct that reported. Tank phoned at 11:30 to say he was conceding the election. Dick thanked him, took Judith's hand, and went out to face the noisy crowd.

The cheering seemed to shake the walls. Dick clasped both hands over his head in a victory gesture. "My friends," he shouted, "I told you I was a fast learner. Apparently, I learned fast enough to convince you that I deserve a second shot at this job. Thank you. I won't let you down."

With that, he left the stage and Connie drove him back to the field office. There was work to do on the new steel import bill before he could call it a day.

Deciding whether to run for reelection is something every member of Congress must decide in the second and final year of their elected term.

Glossary

AMENDMENT. An addition or deletion to a bill.

BILL. A proposed law that will be voted on by the House and Senate

CANDIDATE. Someone who is running for political office.

CAUCUS. A meeting of political party members held for the purpose of deciding policy or selecting candidates.

CONGRESSIONAL RECORD. The Federal Government's printed account of what goes on daily in Congress when it's in session.

CONFERENCE COMMITTEE. A committee made up of members from both houses of Congress. The committee's usual purpose is to compromise differences in bills passed by each house.

CONSTITUENTS. People who live in the district served by congressmen and senators.

EXECUTIVE BRANCH. The branch of government that enforces the law.

FILIBUSTER. An attempt to prevent or delay the passage of a bill.

GENERAL ELECTION. An election in which voters of all parties cast ballots for candidates running for local, state, and national offices.

GERRYMANDER. The practice of dividing a state into legislative districts that favor the party in power.

HEARINGS. Meetings held by a congressional committee for the purpose of gathering information about a bill.

HONORARIUM. A fee paid to a legislator for making a personal appearance.

INCUMBENT. The person who holds a particular office; the term usually refers to someone running for reelection.

JUDICIAL BRANCH. The branch of government that interprets the law.
JUNKET. A trip taken by a legislator which is paid for with public funds. Most junkets mix business with pleasure.

LEGISLATIVE BRANCH. Congress, the branch of government that makes the laws.
LOBBYIST. Someone who tries to influence legislation on behalf of a special interest group.

PARTY LINE VOTE. When lawmakers vote the way their party leaders tell them to vote.
POLITICAL ACTION COMMITTEE (P.A.C.). A committee set up by a special interest group to give money to political candidates.
PORK BARREL. A project voted by Congress that benefits a member's home district. Many porkbarrel projects are wasteful of the taxpayers' money.
PRECINCT. An election district within a city or town.
PRIMARY ELECTION. An election in which members of a political party choose their party's candidates for the general election.

QUORUM CALL. A roll call taken in the House or Senate to see if it has the minimum number of members present.

REDISTRICTING. The redrawing of a state's district boundaries following the ten-year census. Redistricting often leads to gerrymandering by the party in power.

STANDING COMMITTEE. A permanent legislative committee. Each standing committee conducts hearings on bills that fall within its area of expertise.

SUBCOMMITTEE. A subdivision of a legislative committee. Each subcommittee is assigned to study a specific type of legislation.

VETO. The President's power to reject a bill passed by Congress.

Bibliography

Cummings, Frank. *Capitol Hill Manual.* Bureau of National Affairs, Inc., 1984

Fromson, Brett. *Running and Fighting: Working in Washington.* Simon & Schuster, 1981

Gereau, Gerald R., ed. *The Capitol; A Pictorial History of the Capitol and of the Congress.* Government Printing Office, 1981

Goode, Stephen. *The New Congress.* Julian Messner, 1980

How Congress Works. Congressional Quarterly, Inc., 1983

Severn, Bill. *Democracy's Messengers: the Capitol Pages.* Hawthorn Books, 1975

Switzer, Ellen. *There Ought to Be a Law! How Laws Are Made and Work.* Atheneum, 1972

Index

bill *see* legislation

campaigns, campaigning
  finding support, 12-13
  laws governing, 74-78
  raising funds, 12-13, 74-78
Congress
  and the President, 48-49
  committee assignments in, 21-24, 40-44
  committee work, 55-58
  constitutional powers of, 49-51
  dealing with constituents, 31, 36-37, 78, 79
  getting elected to, 11-17
  length of sessions in, 28
  mailing privileges for representatives, 30, 80-81
  offices, 19-21
  qualifications for office, 10, 12
  Rules committee, 65
  rules of conduct in, 52
  seniority system in, 21
  staff duties and size, 18, 58
  voting in, 52-54

ethics, 72-74, 79

gerrymander, 86

laws *see* legislation
legislation
  amending a bill, 67
  and power of committee chairmen, 44
  debate on, 67
  hearings on, 64-65
  introducing a bill to committee, 64-65
  signing, 70-71
  vetoes, 70
  writing of, 62-64
lobbyists, 37-39, 72-74 *see also* PACs

Majority Leader, duties of, 25
Minority Leader, duties of, 25

PACs, 72, 78 *see also* lobbyists

party caucus, 25, 40
party line votes, 44-45
Party Whip, duties of, 25
porkbarrel projects, 45
primary race, 15-16

reelection, running for, 86-89

Speaker of the House, duties of, 25

Picture Credits

Mark Antman/The Image Works	9
AP/Wide World Photos	20, 26-27, 38, 53, 54, 59, 63, 68-69, 83
Tom Ballard/EKM-Nepenthe	87
Copyright Martin Benjamin/The Image Works	50
Alan Carey/The Image Works	34-35
Cathy Cheney/EKM-Nepenthe	19
Copyright Bob Daemmrich/The Image Works	73
Copyright John Maher/EKM-Nepenthe	14
Courtesy of Congressman Christopher Cox	24, 41, 75, 88
Historical Pictures Service, Inc.	46-47
David Valdez/The White House, Courtesy of Congressman Christopher Cox	48